THE FOUR YEAR PLAN

Guaranteed to Get Your Kid Into The Best College

....

Neha Gupta

ISBN 978-1-63443-353-2

Design & Printed by:
3-Keys Graphics & Printing
Pleasanton, CA, USA

NOTE FROM THE AUTHOR

....

My family. Without them, I would not be who I am today. My sister, Shivani, who is my rock on a daily basis. I would also like to thank my coaches Loren Slocum Lahav and Tina Marie Jones for helping me see past my limitations.

My contributing writers: Angela Aie, Bryan Ang, Jordan Ashcraft, Carla Brett, Andrew Crowder, Emily Crowder, Jerry Espinoza, Laura Levilly-Deola, Rafael Lima, Alex Mardock, Gretchen Oertli, Seth Padmabandu and my Elite Private Tutors team.

The goal of this book is to help families understand the importance of preparing ahead. No matter what grade you're in, you can pick up this book and start reading wherever you are in high school. I believe that the entire college admissions process does not need to be stressful. It is important to remember that everything in life happens for a reason. A spiritual teacher once told me to remember to always do your best, and leave the rest.

CONTENTS

....

FOREWORD BY LOREN SLOCUM LAHAV

....

I had the privilege of meeting Neha Gupta at a conference I was facilitating in Fiji a few years ago. I remember the first time I met her. My first response was WOW, a woman with a real sense of purpose! Her certainty, her conviction and her passion for her mission emanated from her.

When she shared about her company, Elite Private Tutors, without hesitation, I remember saying to myself "that's the woman who will understand what my eldest son needs. She will ask great questions to help him feel confident so he knows he is prepared for college.

As a busy mom of a teen, a tween, and a toddler, I am on the road nearly 200 days for my businesses. As much as I love what I do, I love my kids more and am committed to them finding their passion. As we know, life can sometimes be A LOT when you don't have the right resources. I needed to make sure my son had the best resources and I knew Neha was the answer.

The 4 Year Plan will help you as a parent stay grounded in the college decision process so it doesn't feel like you are "nagging" your child, but rather helps you effectively communicate what needs to be done for the best results.

This book makes every step of the process easier to understand the specifics that colleges really want. Giving you tips and secrets for you and your child, The 4 Year Plan will give you the confidence to feel in control and not overwhelmed! Neha and her team have proven success for so many years, they KNOW what you really need. It doesn't require more time, but rather helps you stay calm, save time, and get the RIGHT information. How do I know this to be true? Because that is what it did for my son.

Through the principles in The 4 Year Plan, my son aced his application process. He wrote compelling essays, got amazing referrals, and got accepted to all the colleges he wanted. I am one proud mom. Thanks Neha, your team, and The 4 Year Plan, for making THIS Mom's life so much easier. I wish each of you reading this book, the same!

Stay True,

Loren Slocum Lahav

Mom of a teen, a tween and a toddler, Author of *Life Tune-ups, The Greatest Love, Drama Free Divorce Detox*, Co-Author of *Chicken Soup for the Soul, Time to Thrive, International Speaker and Lifestyle Coach*

WHY READ THIS BOOK?

....

This book is for moms who are their child's number one fan. For moms who are trying their best to give their child everything they need to succeed. This is for all the moms spending late nights organizing binders, and spending countless hours managing their child's iCal schedule. Stop. Stop. Stop. This book is going to help your child create an effective action plan to get into the college of their dreams.

For 12 years I have been coaching kids, and I have picked up on patterns through the thousands of students I have worked with. This book gives both you and your child bite-sized information on all the lessons I have taught students. This book will empower them to earn it for them, instead of you feeling like you are nagging them daily. This book will make your child WANT to pick it up. Sound good?

This isn't the Super Nanny coming in. Students are tired of hearing from their parents, "What do you have due? Let me check your work. Have you filled out your applications?" Wouldn't you love a child who has a sacred place for studying, gets their homework done so they can come down for family dinner with no stress, and takes ownership of their life? Well, if that's the case, let's get started! This book is designed for students of this century who want quick information. While they get most of their information from the latest YouTube video, or creating a Vine video for their friends, or putting their favorite quote on Snap Chat, these children want to absorb information FAST – at lightning speed. They are used to consuming more information than any generation before. So, this book speaks directly to them, since I am also a part of the information generation.

There is a huge level of information in every single chapter. We also give examples of how their actions have consequences by connecting the dots for students to see how their current standards will affect their future. In the end, we want your child to know their strengths, reflect on who they are, and discover what their learning style is, in order to be successful every day in the classroom. So if this sounds like it could help your child win the academic game, this is the right book for you. If not, please give it to a mom who you know could use this to make her life easier.

Now, let's head down the journey of high school onto college dreams. College has become a stressful decision. Many look for name brand colleges, while others search for colleges focused on new careers for the future. Families are realizing that prestige and status-focused colleges are not what the job market is searching for, as it did thirty years ago. The market is looking for candidates with drive, character, and a strong risk appetite. There are so many colleges, and this book will help you succeed month-by-month in high school in order to get into a college that is right for you. There are thousands of colleges beyond the name brand ones that are focused on helping to build the potential of your child, and land them amazing jobs in the future. This book will help open your eyes to the many opportunities beyond high school – but only if you focus on your academic career from 9th through 12th grade. High schools are the foundation of helping you to get into the right college for you!

Remember, a college education nowadays costs almost more than a families' choice of dwelling. This investment is pinnacle in a teenager's development into an adult, where they can find their passion, try new subjects, and explore freedom away from home. So many students forget this, and end up dropping out, getting apathetic in their studies, or transferring to another school.

It takes a village to raise a child, and my goal is to make moms' lives easier every day.

PERSONALITIES OF MOMS

Tiger Mom

This mom is the one who pushes their child to do 8th grade math in 5th grade. The mom who lives vicariously through their child, wanting her child to be the next Steve Jobs or Bill Gates, and will do anything to get them there. This mom is the CEO of her child. This mom wants her child to go to Harvard University, no matter what.

Hands-Off Mom

This mom leaves it up to whatever higher power to decide where her child will end up in college. This mom believes that it is fully the child's responsibility to navigate their academic career. This mom is a co-worker of her child, who doesn't get involved in her child's choices, but comes in when the child is melting down.

I once sat in a session where the mom and I were conversing back and forth about how she needed to be more involved, and she said to me, "It is her job to handle this. I am not dealing with this, she needs to take ownership or just end up in community college." This, of course, was after they paid over $25K per year in private school education for high school!

In-Between Mom

This mom tries to play an advisory role, helping to guide her child to make their own decisions, while giving nuggets of wisdom.

This mom is the consultant. This mom tends to be more balanced in her parenting approach, learning where to step back and let her child fail, and when to step in and pick them up. This mom researches as much as she can to make sure she has the best information for her child. This mom says, "I want him to go to the college of his choice, not because of pressure from me."

Single Mom

This mom is trying to juggle a lot, whether it is work, divorce, her house, or more. Things can slip through the cracks, even though she has the best intentions for her child – and she can't always have it perfectly together. This mom is doing her best being the CEO of her house, CEO of her family, and CEO of her own mental sanity.

This mom is trying to stay afloat with the academic game. She needs an efficient resource to help her know what to do to navigate her child's ups and downs, and all the important deadlines. This mom is trying her best to stay on top of her list, but also has the best interests of her child in mind, even if she is going through a lot.

Mom That is Still in High School

This mom is going to Office Depot on her own, picking out her favorite Jonathan Adler planner, studying the online school schedule, and putting the dates in for her child. This mom is filling out her child's college applications when the time comes, and organizing her binders during midterms and finals. This mom is the employee of her child.

This mom is someone I come across often. "I just finished organizing his binders, since he was too tired from football last night. Here are the notes organized in stacks, and here is the application I filled out for him for this school." This mom has no idea that she is setting her child up for failure their first year in college, even though she has the child's absolute best interests at heart. These moms can sometimes suffer from being too perfect in their mindset, and not letting their child take ownership of who they need to be to get to the right college for them.

Combo Mom

Now there is, of course, the designer breed. Know that we are all a combo of the few listed above. It doesn't make you less or better. I put this together for you to see the different strategies and approaches. This mom tends to have a bit of everything in her, and shines these personalities at different times. She is still the number one fan of her child, and uses each of the strategies—at the right time, or the wrong time—to get that across. At the end of the day, she just loves her child and wants to do what is best.

PERSONALITIES OF STUDENTS

....

Sporty Student

This student is highly committed compared to most of the entire student body. Dedicating close to 10 to 12 hours a week can be challenging, and only a select few can balance this with high honors courses and AP courses. With a demanding schedule, many of these students can flounder when dealing with harder classes that take much more time to study for in their junior and senior years. This student gets home around six, tired and hungry. Schoolwork can literally break this student, after being outside on the field for two hours every day.

Nerd

This student is in all honors and AP courses. They are in the game, and deep in the game. Sometimes this student suffers from extreme levels of stress and anxiety with the levels of self-pressure they put on themselves, that might not even come from their parents. These students are front-row clients, and they smile brightly at the teacher in every class. These students expect themselves to be all-A students, and harp on a 95 instead of a 100 on their last Bio AP test. These students are present after school, talking to teachers about things that are relevant to their subject. They are calculating their GPA after every single test to make sure they are still in the top 10%.

Overly Organized

This student has the best level of organization and time management system set up, so they know exactly what they are doing. This student is focused on making sure every single letter they write is perfectly written, and sometimes they get bogged down by the details. Being so perfect at their system, they can be slower to get things done. This student knows exactly what it takes to prepare for a final, and sometimes can re-write all their notes to make sure they are perfect, instead of studying.

Unmotivated Student

This student, simply, does not care about school. They think it is a means to an end. They want to take five steps ahead and be the next Mark Zuckerberg. These students tend to sit in the back of the class and are too busy iChatting their friends about the latest movie launch. They are not interested in the material, and tend to feel that they are focused on how they look or when the next party is. This student does not realize the detriment they are causing to their future by making the decision to not focus on their academic career. They also tend to have all of their papers crammed into the bottom of their backpack. This might seem harsh, but this is an important student to focus on. There are a lot of issues that cause a child to check out. This student tends to have potential that is just not unleashed yet. This student could have been bullied, or had a bad experience in a class. As coaches, we try to find out what happened five minutes ago or five years ago, as you never know what is going on with them until you ask the right question.

One of the students I worked with was extremely apathetic toward school. Prior to high school, she was doing well in her middle school, but after dealing with some family issues, transitioning to a new school, and all the new rules of high school, her grades suffered. She was unable to keep up with the speed of coursework and hours of basketball practice. After focusing on a set strategy with her, she was able to get into the honor roll, and find herself quickly. Many students think 9th grade is about gearing up, but that should really be happening during the summer prior.

Artistic Student

This student tends to daydream, and dream in bright colors. This student has paint on her skirt, and tends to be extremely creative when it comes to projects. This student loves to do art or theater, and can be a bit dramatic at times. They are passionate and eccentric, and they love hard. At the same time, if they do not like a subject, they feel very forced. This student tends to run their lives based on passion.

I Can't Do It Student

Some students are told that they are just not good at "X" subject. Or, that they will always be a "B or C" student. Assigning a child an identity where they feel they are "less than" is one of the biggest ways to harm a student's self-confidence. I had a student who was unable to do well in Spanish, because she constantly told herself she could not do well in languages. Having this belief trumped her ability to push past it and develop the tenacity that is needed when faced with a challenge. After working together, we were able to raise her grades, but one of the main focuses of our sessions was confidence building.

WHY START EARLY?

One of the biggest mistakes parents make is starting this entire process during senior year. So many students do not have a plan! Schools are trying to teach students and get them good grades. Guidance counselors are trying to help too many students with the college process, and they're unable to handle the detailed questions from parents about their unique situation. Parents are trying to keep up financially with paying for every activity for their child, and parent their child, while staying happily married. It isn't the same as when they were in school. Just with the Internet alone, the game has changed to online applications. Parents are trying to understand the entire game of applying to college, because it is night and day from when they applied – submitting an application in an envelope. Everyone is trying to keep up, and it is so hard to keep up with information overload. Wouldn't you like to know the order of priority of how to successfully prepare for college?

WHY I LOVE THE COLLEGE CONSULTING PROCESS

I had a child who had gone through extreme physical abuse from her mom. Her mom suffered from drug abuse. When we wrote the child's essay, she was able to heal many of her wounds by telling her story. Later, she read her essay to the entire student body, and they were able to really celebrate her for moving forward in life and being able to tell her authentic story. College essays are about taking the time to dig deep and talk about serious issues or lessons you have endured during high school. Although this story of my student is extremely raw, there are hundreds of stories I have uncovered while working with children on their college essays.

9TH GRADE

HOW TO GET ORGANIZED FOR HIGH SCHOOL

....

Long gone are the days of pretty colored paper, fill in the blank notes, and teachers that hold your hand like they did in middle school. Welcome to high school, baby, where you are being prepped for college starting DAY ONE. As someone who attended one of the top universities, Rice University, I would say even at a top private college-prep high school, I still wasn't prepared for what Rice threw at me. So, let me give you the lowdown on how important it is to learn how to get organized from day one in high school.

This is one of the major reasons why my company, Elite Private Tutors exists. Students cannot get themselves organized, to the point where we now offer Organizational Coaching as a separate service in order to help students understand the important of breaking down homework, having a planner, and organizing their binders. A disorganized binder is as bad as wearing the same underwear all week. I know that is extreme and disgusting, but the ones who succeed are the ones who have figured this out. I have YET to see a top ten student who has crumpled paper in their backpack, zeros for homework because they couldn't find it, or doesn't have some form of an organizational planner tool.

Speaking of, let's talk about the planner. Since all of you are now in the tech age, you all seem to think a planner (one which your mom buys in cute colors for herself), is SO old-school. Who would pull out a little book to check their calendar, when their iPhone, iMac, and iPad can sync their calendar events perfectly? Also, with schools embracing technology and teachers SLOWLY adding their assignments to the portal, you are starting to rely heavily on technology to stay organized. Since I am not that much older than you, and went to a laptop school when laptops weighed more than a ten-pound dumbbell, I understand this generation extremely well. So, let me give you a few options.

Written Planner

The written planner that your school provides usually has specific school holidays listed in it. You can use it to write down your homework at the end of every class. Many of the students I work with say, "I have so little time between the bell ringing and getting to the next class, I can't do that." Well, my suggestion is to find the time. I cannot tell you the number of times a student has no idea what is due, and is frantic that evening. They check the portal, and many teachers have NOT adopted the online portal, even if it is required of them!

Writing things down has been useful since the days of papyrus paper. It offers calendar views, which you should fill out the DAY you get your syllabus, and it has all the quiz and test dates listed. In addition, if you get a monthly calendar from your class, please add it to this planner. Do not try to stay organized by looking at six calendars separately in each binder—that is ridiculous. You will miss something. That's like cooking a meal with six different cookbooks

–it won't be a great meal. It takes literally 15 minutes to this, and it helps you to plan out your semester.

iCal, online solutions, iProcrastinate and Google Calendars

Many students will sync their school portal with their iCal. This works, except that every time I work with a student, they always miss stuff because there are still archaic teachers that REFUSE to update their calendar. FYI: It is STILL not your teachers' job to update you on what is due, through your online system. It is YOUR job to do this, as it will be for the rest of your life. When you get older, no one is going to tell you to shower, get out of bed for work, and go be a rockstar. So don't expect your teachers to do this for you.

I am a serious user of iCal, because I am someone who plans out my life months in advance – it really is the only way to live the kind of life I do, where I travel so much, have work and family obligations, and add fun to my life. So, I am a believer in iCal and I have someone whose sole job is to manage it for me and confirm every appointment for me.

For you, iCal can be extremely helpful in making sure that you are set on your dates for quizzes, tests, and papers – and you can see it in month view, week view, and day view. My favorite is how the iPad sets it up. You can also set up your evening between 4 and 10 p.m. with the estimated time you think it will take to do your homework, so you have a plan of action instead of a six-hour blob of time in the evening where you watch reality TV and eat junk food, and then realize that you didn't open your backpack until 9 p.m.

Stickies

Absolutely not. I never recommend this. People do not become successful planning their lives on stickies. My mother does this, and she literally forgets what time her flight is (she missed her flight for X-mas), doctor's appointments, and so much more in life. She misses friends' parties, and it makes them think she is flakey. She is also a serial entrepreneur, and it can really affect her business that she doesn't have ONE system—it is actually kind of weird how she operates, in my opinion.

Anyway, enough about my mother. I know all of you have LOADS of opinions about yours, so don't judge me. Stickies are stupid. It's as stupid as writing a note to yourself in pen on your hand, and then you wash your hands all day and lose it. So, do not use this system. It does not give you a BIG PICTURE view of your semester whatsoever. It tells you what you need to get done that same day, or a quick note for remembering to buy something, or that you need to text your mom at lunchtime. This is not an organizational tool.

Using your Body as an Organizational Tattoo

First, you look like an idiot. Unless you are writing your digits on a girl or boy in your twenties, writing on yourself is so '90s. Move on from it, and use a pen or your thumbs on a technological device.

I am personally a combo user of iCal and a written planner. I can't remember the last time I wrote on a body of any sort, whether it was mine or someone else's. When you get older, it changes from subjects to To-Do lists comprised of personal and work lists. So get with it, buddy!

Binder Organization

Holy moly, guys. Some of your binders look like you stuffed it into the most powerful blender you could find and hit the power button. Or you stuck it in a Texas-sized tornado and then it flew into your backpack. What is going on? Do you think the assignments you are given are useless? Let me tell you the horror of tornado binders, as I call them.

I was working with a student named David recently, who literally had English, Science and History mixed up randomly into three binders. Holy crap. I am giving you the breakdown on how this works, even though I know you have probably heard it in homeroom or advisory, and chose to listen to the latest track on iTunes instead. Binders – get the flexible ones, and don't buy cheap ones. I have seen students bust a binder and it's game over, so don't try to skimp on binders. I know they are expensive, but buy ones that are going to last you at least 8 months. Either buy 2 to 3 large ones to hold a few subjects in each, or smaller ones for each subject.

To be honest, this depends on if you go to your locker or not. There is this horrible trend of students carrying all their binders in their backpacks as a walking locker. Welcome to chiropractic care, spinal doctors, and massage therapy, kids – this will WRECK your spine. So, RUN to your locker. Most students need the exercise anyway, based on the current childhood obesity rates and the fact that you sit at A DESK ALL DAY.

Dividers

I suggest the ones with the folders – for the occasional stuffing right when the bell rings, or for the dreaded teacher that seems to not know what a hole puncher is. These come in a range of colors. You can even label and print them out on your computer in fun little fonts if you want to go crazy – please do.

Divider Tab Names: Syllabus, Notes, Quizzes, Tests, Papers (English, History), Labs (Science), Handouts

Most teachers try to enforce you to have binders that are organized by doing binder checks. Honestly, the reason I am a tutor is because I would be the most comical teacher on the planet, with the harshest grading. Well, that's a lie. I recently graded everyone 110 on their science fair projects in 8th grade because I liked the way they did their board, or their ability to communicate effectively, or that they have a great idea. So, maybe I wouldn't be the harshest grader. But I would definitely focus on life skills more than class material, so binder checks would be instilled literally on a weekly basis. It's like maintaining your weight—you can't eat four McDonald's burgers in one week and think you won't have to pay for it later. So, organized binders – super important.

I love, love, love when I hear this: "Girls are organized, and boys just have a hard time with this." What a lame-o excuse, people. I will admit, I do work mostly with boys on organization, but this is not an excuse, men. Let me tell you a little secret your mom won't tell you. When you are in your late twenties and date grown women, and you seem to have FORGOTTEN the time or when you scheduled a date, it does NOT matter how many millions you make, or the fact that you have some cool, awesome. She will NEVER go out with you again, and if you stood her up once, consider it done. So organization should be TOP on your list. Plus, it shows up in your work life, both girls and boys – and the ones that are the most task-oriented and organized succeed the most. If you aren't, you will have co-workers constantly suggesting to you how to get organized. So, get with it.

OTHER FUN SCHOOL SUPPLIES

Pens

I love Uniball – such a great investment. Or Le Pen – I discovered these in 9th grade when my teacher, Mrs. G, made it a requirement to draw the entire world, with all the countries and capitals, from memory with these pens. Yeah, guys, school was HARDER back then – she can't even assign this anymore, since students seem to Google everything and refuse to learn what they consider mindless info. Guess what? As someone who gets 8 to 10 stamps in their passport every year now, this assignment still helps. Thanks, Mrs. G – you rock. Just make sure you find a pen that you like and doesn't smear.

Pencils

I am not a fan of the No. 2 pencil unless you are using it for a Scantron. It's messy and it gets all over the place. Get the cute mechanical ones that look like wannabe pencils.

Binder holepuncher

This is a lifesaver. I recommend it for every student on this planet. It literally lets you holepunch anything on the go – and it's super thin. Whoever made this probably made millions and is sitting on some beach in Mexico somewhere.

Paper

I am constantly scrounging around for paper during my tutoring sessions. Sometimes I want to start etching my suggestions on their arms as punishment for not having enough supplies for me. I work with elite students who can most definitely afford a pack of paper, yet it seems like all I have to work with is a pen, with no paper. I know we are technologically in an age of laptops, but you WILL need paper for school. So choose between college ruled and wide-ruled. My suggestion is wide-ruled, but that's because I like space in my notes. Or get college ruled, and write on every other line.

Calculator

Don't forget this for a math test. That's just plain stupid. Plus, calculators now are practically mini-laptops.

For all of you who hate to read, or want things in 160 characters or less, here is the short, list version of what I just said, without all the hilarious jokes.

- Binders – Flexible Ones

- Dividers – roughly 5-6 per subject, preferably with folders

- Pens – Uniball or Le Pen

- Pencils – Mechanical and a few No. 2s

- Paper – wide or college ruled, depending on you preference

- Calculator – important for math, you have to take it all four years

HOW TO STUDY FOR HIGH SCHOOL EXAMS

....

It shocks me how many students do not know how to study for tests. It's as if they were picked off some island near Timbuktu and never attended middle school. Students, the teachers literally give you everything you need in 9th grade to get an A. It's like they hand it to you on a platter. Wait till 11th grade, when they say, "Review sheet? Who are you? Go back to 9th grade." Or wait until college, where every time you step into a one-hour class, you are going over an ENTIRE chapter in the book, and your tests cover 7 chapters, which equates to your cumulative final at the end of the year in 9th grade. So, studying for tests is a skill you'd better learn FAST.

Here is my recipe for success. Before a test, TOP students do not study hours before, the morning of, the all-nighter before, or even a day or two prior. They are studying at least a minimum of 4 days prior to the test. Don't let these "smart" kids fool you by saying, "Dude, I barely opened my backpack and made like a 96." Or, as many of my honors students would say, "Oh yeah, that was like so easy, I barely study." Study the bags under their eyes, they totally study hours upon hours. Don't compare yourself to anyone else. Most students either HIGHLY exaggerate stress levels and anxiety attacks, or try to down play it by implying they were born like Albert Einstein or something.

Study at least 4 days to a week prior to the test. Especially if it is for science or history. Actually, I take that back: for all subjects. Get your notes organized based on the material from the last test date to the new test date. Organize them chronologically (they should already be chronologically ordered in your binder, FYI). Pull them out and paperclip them together. Then, look at any quizzes you took during the time from the last test to this test. MOST TEACHERS COPY QUIZ QUESTIONS FOR THEIR TESTS. As someone in their twenties, if I wanted to have an awesome killer life and teach high schoolers, I would also copy the questions over, because I don't feel the need to be THAT creative. Plus, 90% of students don't know this secret, or don't care to abide by it. SO CORRECT YOUR QUIZZES IMMEDIATELY AFTER YOU GET THEM BACK. And then memorize those questions and answers, baby!

All of those tonado binder students get B's and C's specifically for this reason: they can't find their quizzes, and therefore they don't even have the opportunity. Also, don't think you can find some cute guy or girl to continually copy stuff from. Students are highly competitive these days.

Okay, back to how to study for a test. Start reviewing your notes. Make notecards for key terms, dates, important vocabulary, people that are important, etc. These will be used for your reviews for midterms and finals – you are incrementally setting yourself up for success for the entire year. Most of my students try to make notecards online using Quizlet. I don't know how many times I have to explain this to students, but I am going to repeat myself again for the 12,000th time.

Here is a little story: Do you remember that text you sent two minutes ago while you were reading this book? I mean like, every single word of it? Do you remember that hand-written card you wrote to someone, or that someone wrote to you? WHICH ONE DO YOU REMEMBER BETTER? Guys, we are visual people, and we're kinesthetic learners. That's just a fancy way of saying the combination of seeing something and feeling it at the same time is KILLER for human beings in the learning sector. So writing stuff down instead of typing is EPIC.

I type roughly 98 to 100 words per minute. I barely remember what I wrote in the last chapter because I type so fast. The connection between hand-writing, seeing something, and recalling something in your brain helps you learn faster, which in the end is one of the most important skills learned in high school, due to the level of information you have to consume. Unless you have a photographic memory, don't try to use it as the only study method.

So, now you have your chronologically ordered notes, your notecards andyour corrected quizzes. Make sure you also pull any relevant handouts, and find out after school what is relevant on the test. Ask early on – showing interest a week ahead to a teacher signals that you care. And in the end, teachers are SUCKERS for that. I am a top tutor, and when I see a student taking the extra mile, I talk and gab about them to my friends, brag about them to my family, and help them so much more. So do most teachers. They just act all cool about it because they can't have favorites!

HOW TO PREPARE FOR MIDTERMS

....

November is the last full month of class before midterms. Now, maybe you had midterms in middle school, but high school midterms will probably be different in format—and much harder! Hopefully, during this semester you were keeping up with each new lesson in your classes, but if you got behind at any point, this is the opportunity to catch up, especially during Thanksgiving break. The tests you will have at the end of the semester will cover everything from August, which is no small task!

Preparing now in November will help you tremendously during December, when you sit down to the test reviews. Now is the time to start going back the material and make sure you understand them. When you sit down to start this process, it can be overwhelming. All of the notes, quizzes, and tests...where do I start?

Notecards

Here's another pro tip: say the terms out loud as you write them down and define them. The combination of writing and saying the words will help you process the terms even more, and will help you to memorize them.

Just a re-review on notecards. For classes with tons of memorization, like Biology, History, and Language classes, you'll likely need the cards.

In the month of November, you'll have something to look forward to: Thanksgiving Break. As you prepare to stuff your face with turkey, you can also be taking time to prepare for finals. Showing discipline during the break will definitely pay off. Most students start studying after Thanksgiving break. You can give yourself an edge by starting over the break.

Wait – I know what you're thinking again: "But why would they call it a break if I should be doing work?!" You should definitely give yourself some time to relax while you don't have school, but there is enough time for both. Relax, eat pie, watch football, and spend time with your family on Thanksgiving, but do so knowing that you have spent some time working on your most difficult subject on the days leading up to Thanksgiving, and knowing that you should continue for the rest of the break.

Now that I've convinced you to give up some of your videogame time during Thanksgiving break for studying, let's set up a game plan. Look ahead to the midterms you are dreading the most: midterms for the most difficult class, the class you hate or the class that needs a grade boost. These are the classes you should start with, so that you have the foundation built when you start studying again in December. For these classes, start from the beginning. Hopefully, you have been keeping up with your binders, so when you sit down to start looking at lessons from August, you'll flip right to what you need. Starting with the earliest lessons—yes, even the ones from the first week that seemed really simple—go back and review the concepts.

For math and science classes, work through old homework problems for practice. Once you've completed several correctly, move on to the next lesson. Working diligently, you should be able to get through a serious chunk of the class.

For reading-based classes, like History or English, get out that pile of notecards that we talked about earlier this month. Go back through them and compare them to the notes you have for the class. When you're done, congratulate yourself on taking the initiative, because most of your classmates didn't even touch their backpacks! Preparing now will make December so much less stressful! Make sure to map out 30-40 minutes per day to study for each midterm up until that test. It will give you roughly 12 hours per class to review over 100 hours of material.

HOW TO CREATE STUDY SPACES WITH FEWER DISTRACTIONS AT HOME

....

Studying is hard. Or at least, students find it to be one of the hardest things about being in high school. Something about coming home after a long day at school, and cracking open a textbook to study for a test the next day is just unappealing. In fact, everything about that scenario is unappealing. However, it's something every student has to do, and it will only be a burden to you if you think of it as one. Especially today, with all the technology, it's so much easier to procrastinate and watch TV, go on the Internet, or text your friends. Anything to put off studying just a minute longer.

Studying is only difficult if you make it difficult. Now don't get me wrong, there will be difficult tests. If you got by in middle school without studying for a single test and think the same strategy will fly in high school, think again. But don't be intimidated! Just like anything else, there are always strategies that will help make studying just a little bit easier.

First off, you need to find an environment that is best suited for you to study. This depends entirely on you! Some people prefer silence and like to study in a library. Others really like coffee shops and bookstores. Remember, there's always the easiest location - your house! Also keep in mind that all of these places can have their own distractions, so it's up to you to find the one that is best for you, where you have minimal distractions and the best focus.

One thing that I will always say about doing homework and studying is to find a desk or table - some kind of surface. Don't do your studying lying in bed or curled up on a couch. Take it from someone who has tried this. You are going to fall asleep! It's going to happen at one point or another. With just the right (or wrong, depending on how you look at it) amount of bad luck, it'll end up being for a test you really need to study for, and you won't wake up until the next morning when it's time for school. Use a desk! Sit upright with your books and notes open, and put away all your other distractions. There can be plenty of these places in your house, such as an office or even the kitchen table. It's recommended that you don't study in the same room that you sleep in, but if your desk is in there, it's completely fine.

Your study environment is what you make of it, so make sure that it works for you! If you find yourself unable to work at your house, go to a local Starbucks, or maybe the library if you want a more quiet study space. There are so many options that you can tailor to your individual needs.

The biggest problems students have while studying is distractions. Cell phones, laptops, tablets, TV - so much technology to distract you from work and give you an excuse to keep procrastinating. Put it away! There are many students that take hours to study material that could have been learned in less than an hour if there were no distractions, because they are constantly wasting time on their computer, picking up their phone every time they got a message, or one of the worst distractions in my opinion - watching TV while studying. Don't get me wrong. I love watching TV shows as much as the next person. One of the best and worst feelings is spending hours binge watching a new show you just discovered on Netflix. But, like everything, there's a time and a place. And the time for you to be on Netflix is definitely not when you have a test coming up. Resist the temptation! It is so much more rewarding to relax after you know you aced a test than it is to procrastinate, which leads to unnecessary stress.

There is absolutely no reason that the TV should be on while you are working. It gives you no benefit at all, so do yourself a favor and just turn it off, finish your work, and then watch TV if you have the time. It's 2014. If you really want to see a show, record it and watch it later! Stream it online at a more convenient time for you. It serves no purpose other than to distract you, and every scientific study done supports the idea that your brain functions much better when the TV is off. Both studies and common sense tell us this, and yet so many students make this mistake.

Another big distraction, especially in recent years, is cell phones and texting. You are not benefitting from picking up your phone every 10 seconds to shoot your friends a text. Communication is so fast-paced today that texting your friends all day has become the norm. However, you see them all day at school, and for many of you over the weekends as well. Just put it on silent and set it down while you study, or give it to your parents with the condition that you get it back once you're finished studying. Or, set it aside and only check your messages after you've read a certain number of pages, or completed a certain number of problems.

Putting your phone down and having a little time to yourself will do you some good beyond just studying better. Even if you're not studying, sometimes just putting your phone on silent and having 20 minutes of peace to yourself can go a long way to improving your day.

As far as friends go, as much as we all love our friends, we know how much of a distraction they can be. Who wants to decline their friends' invitation to hang out in favor of studying for a test? The unfortunate truth is, it has to be done. Learn to say no to your friends sometimes. It's completely okay to say, "No, I can't hang out today. I have to study for the math test tomorrow." It may suck at the moment, when you are stuck studying and your friends are having fun, but when you get that test grade back, you will know your decision was completely worth it. It's going to happen even more from here on out. In college and after, your friends will have different priorities at different times. It's up to you to set your priorities straight and learn when you've got to buckle down, bite the bullet, and hit the books.

"I study better with music." This is another distraction that a lot of people find very controversial. A lot of people out there claim that they study better with music, as you see them reading with headphones in. The truth is, this probably isn't true, even if they think it is. I personally cannot have any music playing. In fact, if I am reading, I need almost absolute silence. Otherwise I can't focus. I once took the batteries out of a ticking clock because the ticking noises made it impossible for me to concentrate (a very extreme example of noise distractions, but you get the idea). Most people aren't this sensitive to noise when studying, but to an extent everyone's brain is distracted by outside noise. Even if you like to study with music, I strongly encourage you to try without it. I can almost guarantee that you will remember more information if you study with silence than if you have music playing in the background. It'll definitely be worth it when you're taking a test and the answer to the question pops into your head, instead of the lyrics to the song you were listening to when you were studying that topic.

On the opposite end of the spectrum of not working enough is working too hard. Believe it or not, studying for too long can actually hurt your productivity. Yes, you read correctly. Studying for too long at one time can actually be a distraction! It is completely okay to take breaks. In fact, it's highly encouraged. If you don't take breaks, you will burn out early in the night, especially if you have a lot of studying ahead of you. Research shows the best form of studying is twenty-five minutes of work, followed by a five-minute break. By twenty-five minutes of work, I mean vigorous work. This means no phone, no computer, just you and your book and notes. This doesn't mean that you can browse Facebook for twenty minutes, work for five, and then take a break. You've got to earn that break! One suggestion is downloading the app Pomodoro – it helps you take more breaks!

Sleep! The one thing that everybody loves is sleep. It's wonderful. And you need it. You shouldn't have to pull all-nighters regularly if you are effectively managing your time. A sleep-deprived brain is perhaps the greatest distraction of all. When you're tired, you can't think properly, you won't remember as much information, and you definitely won't perform as well on an exam as you would if you had gotten adequate rest the night before. There comes a time when the benefit of sleep outweighs the benefit of studying, and you just need to go to bed. It's really up to you when this is, and it depends on how much you have already studied and how much sleep you need as an individual (I personally need 9 hours, which is totally impractical, and I have learned to deal with 8). The recommended amount for high school students is 7 to 8 hours. When you are tired, it's your body sending you a message. Listen to it.

Always remember that although you want to cut out these distractions while you study, you don't want to necessarily cut out the "distractions" from your life completely. You need to have something that takes your mind off school and lets you relax. While prioritizing your school work and studies at a very high level, always be sure to take some time for yourself, too. Go out, hang out with your friends, have some fun! Sprawl out on the couch and binge watch some Netflix (but only when you don't have studying to do). Enjoy yourself during high school as much as you work hard. It seems like a long time, but I promise by the end of it you'll wonder where those four years went.

Do's and Don'ts for Studying to Eliminate Distractions

DO

- Have a positive attitude about studying. If you dread studying, you are going to view it as a burden and hate every minute of it.

- Find something that you enjoy doing. For instance, if you find yourself liking your history class, then studying for that class will be a positive experience for you.

- Take breaks. It's a distraction to you if your brain isn't working at its full capability.

- Get some sleep! Sleep deprivation is one of the biggest distracters out there!

- Enjoy yourself. Remember, life isn't all about work. You need to relax and unwind sometimes. Enjoy your time in high school. It only comes once, and you'll be wondering where the time went when it's over.

- Download Pomodoro for taking breaks.

DON'T

- Overwork yourself. Know your limitations. Push yourself, but don't do anything that is hazardous to your health. This includes overwork and sleep deprivation.

- Turn the TV off. There is no reason for you to be watching TV while you are studying. It's just distracting. I can't stress this enough!

- Constantly be using your phone or your computer. Put them away while you study, and you'll find yourself to be much more productive.

- Listen to loud music.

- Ditch studying for friends.

HOW TO START THE SEMESTER OFF RIGHT

....

After the winter break, classes start again in January. You've eaten plenty of pie and caught up on sleep. Now it's time to get the spring semester started off on the right foot. Here are some tips for making sure that the semester is smooth sailing - right into summer break.

Go back with a positive attitude, knowing you have a fresh start on grades.

Almost no one wants to go back to school so quickly after the new year starts, but there isn't a choice, so you should make the best of it. Going back to school for a new semester means that you have a clean slate with your grades for this semester. If there were any grades that you weren't happy with last semester, you can change them for the better when you start fresh. Leave the past behind you and get motivated to do better.

Don't slack off at the beginning of the semester.

The beginning of the semester seems easy, as teachers ease you back into schoolwork. This does not mean you should slack off and get behind on work, because the lessons only get harder as you go through the semester. Finals will be incredibly hard if you decide not to put in the work now.

Take advantage of the lighter load to get ahead.

This is the time to focus on any problem areas in your schedule. For instance, if you struggled with Geometry last semester, you can spend the free time you have ensuring that you are up to date on all lessons from the previous semester, and look ahead to any lessons that seem particularly difficult.

Planning at the start of the semester is crucial to your success throughout it, but the best planning comes from evaluating the results you had the last time around. At the beginning of the semester, you should take some time to reflect on the last semester, looking at what worked and what didn't. And don't be afraid to ask others for help in your reflection! Some of my best ideas and realizations come from talking with my friends, family and teachers about how they thought I handled certain things, and they always have valuable new ideas to try! You can always hire an Elite Edge Coach too!

Playing to your strengths for the coming semester will ensure that you have a successful one. To set you up, here are just a few of the things you should reflect on.

Grades

Was I happy with all of my grades? If not, which ones? What could I have done to get better ones? Do I have a good foundation for the material moving forward into the class this semester? Do I need to think about getting a tutor EARLY for subjects I may have struggled with?

Organization

Did I keep up with my planner last semester? Did I ever forget assignments or important due dates, and why? Was it easy to find notes and review sheets when it was time to study? Did I have an organized, quiet study space at home? If no is the answer to any of these, what can I do to make this happen now?

Time Management

Did I have enough time to accomplish everything I wanted last semester (including plenty of sleep)? Which activities outside of class took up the most time? Which ones are most important to me? Were there any particularly stressful periods during the semester, and why were they stressful? Did I stick to the study and homework schedules I made? If having enough time to get things done was an issue, how can I schedule more effectively?

January is a very important time of year to make goals! It is a common cliché to make New Years' resolutions, but setting goals is an important part of starting the semester off right. The first step to setting goals is to look back at the previous semester. What do you wish you had done better? Academically, look at how your classes went last semester. How did your grades turn out? Is there a class that you felt you could have done better in? Luckily, most high school classes are set up in two-semester courses, so you have the opportunity to do better in the spring semester. I don't mean you should simply think about what you could do better: physically write down the goals you have.

For example, if you were disappointed with your grade in Biology, don't simply say, "I will do better in Biology this semester." Instead, say: "I didn't like that I had an 82 in Biology last semester. I would really like to get an A. My goal is to have at least a 90 average by the end of the semester." Remember, goals should be specific and realistic. For example, if you got a C- in a class last semester, perhaps setting your sights on a B would be more attainable. Your goal should be a reflection of what you believe is the best you can do if you put forth your best effort. This does NOT mean: what your parents think you can do, what your parents expect of you, or what you could get if you put in a half-effort. These goals should come from YOU. What you think you can feasibly do if you try your hardest and submit your best work.

This strategy for setting goals does not simply apply to your academic life. In general, school should be going well in all aspects, including clubs, sports, and friends. The same technique for making academic goals applies to these elements as well. How involved are you outside of classes? If last semester was too stressful, consider breaking from a club this semester. Were you too intimidated in the first semester to join anything? Set the goal to go outside of your comfort zone. Take some time to look at your life as a high school student so far, and prepare yourself for the next seven semesters. With goals, you can get the most out of the experience.

EXAMPLE GOALS LIST

- Raise Biology grade from 82 to 90 by making notecards and visiting the teacher weekly.

- Join the Students of Services Club and volunteer 3 times this semester.

- Try to take the lead on a project.

- Drop a sport.

- Work on my writing skills for English class.

- Try to be more enthusiastic about Geometry.

- Look at my History teacher with fresh eyes.

HOW TO DO ABROAD SERVICE TRIPS

....

One of the best experiences to broaden your worldview and educate you on other cultures and social issues—not to mention strengthen your resume- is going on some a service trip abroad. These trips can be terrifying at first (especially for your parents) because they will undoubtedly push you out of your comfort zone, but it is also part of the growing process.

Service abroad trips give you a unique opportunity to walk in the shoes of other people and understand the daily challenges they face. For most people, these trips fill them with gratitude for what they have, make them more aware of global, social, and justice issues, and uncover an issue or world problem that you might feel passionate about. And as icing on the cake of your personal growth and development, admissions committees love to see service abroad on applications, and how it has impacted your life.

The summer after my freshman year, I did a week-long mission trip to a town right across the border in Mexico. We stayed at a church, and mainly worked to help the community with whatever needs presented themselves. We cleaned up debris from fallen houses, painted houses, removed a roof and installed a new one, served food in the soup kitchen, sorted items in their donation store, and played with kids from the community at night. We ate authentic

Mexican food (which was so yummy!) and I even got to try out a little of my Spanish.

It was an eye-opening experience to see the differences not only in our cultures, but in the hardships life handed to the people we worked with. The things that seemed all-important at school, like who's dating who, and who's wearing what, paled in comparison to the daily struggle to find shelter and food. It was an experience that taught me that I wanted to make a tangible difference in peoples' lives, and it started me on a journey to figuring out just how I could do that.

So now that you've decided you want to embark on an abroad service trip, there are a few things you need to consider. First, start considering your trip options by finding organizations that lead service trips. Churches often have one or two summer trips that they lead, or they can put you in touch with people who are leading trips. Also, check out high school service organizations that sometimes plan trips, and lastly, use the Internet.

There are an overwhelming number of service organizations out there who also focus on working with specific issues, such as clean water, poverty, human trafficking, or education. It can be harder to go through an organization you don't have any experience with, so when choosing a trip this way, do the following:

• Be sure to find as many details as possible

• Ask questions directly to the people leading the trip

- See how organized the trip is

- See how well planned out the activities are

- Find out what connections the organization has to the place you'll be working in

- Do they have past experience in this location?

- What plans do they have in case of emergencies while abroad? Safety is the number one priority, so you should be able to ask as many questions as you need to feel secure.

The reason I suggest you start thinking about this in February, is that there is a lot of planning and work beforehand. Besides planning for passports and visas if the host country requires it, there will often be fundraising involved to offset the high cost of the trip. Starting to plan early will leave you and your parents plenty of time to plan every little detail out, which will help you have a safer and more productive trip, and will help relieve your parents' anxiety - although not all of it, because they will worry no matter what!

HOW TO FOCUS ON COMMUNITY SERVICE

....

Whenever I think of community service, I usually think of having to work without pay. Doesn't seem very fun, does it? Or could it be? One summer my mom wanted me to participate in a volunteer service called City Ministries. The thought of spending my Christmas vacation "working" did not sound fun to me at all. But I took a deep breath and let out a sigh that slowly agreed to her plea. I couldn't understand it at the time, but later I did.

Early morning I woke up to the sound of my alarm clock. It was time for my first day at City Ministries. I walked inside and saw tons of gifts, food, and people. It was a bit overwhelming. As I stood while the guy spoke of our duties at orientation, my eyes drifted to all the marvelous gifts. I thought in my head, "Wow, I can't believe someone donated all of this great stuff." When orientation was over, it was time to get started. I was placed in the sorting department, where I gathered toys for different ages of children.

After a long few hours of placing things in the right sections, a lady approached me and it was time to hand out gifts to families. I walked to my new station, where I saw this family who looked worn down. They appeared as if this was their last hope at a good holiday. The children playing unknowingly of the situation captured my eye. I thought to myself, I am doing something amazing. I am helping to give this family a happy memory.

When I went home later that day, I felt a great feeling of success. I helped people that couldn't help themselves. I didn't know it at the time, but this event helped me in ways more than I can describe. It helped me grow. This is why I feel that community service is such an important part of high school, and going forth into college. Look into a community service project that you will enjoy. If you are one of those people who feel they can't quite find the right volunteer service for you, that's okay. I still want you to get out there and pick one. Take me, for example. I never thought I would enjoy helping out at the place I did, but it rewarded me in more ways than I could imagine.

9th Grade · April

HOW TO STUDY FOR FINALS

···

The whole school year has passed, and now it feels like you are faced with a final in every class. Do not fear, however, because I will teach you the perfect strategy for passing all your finals with flying colors. Contrary to what you expect, you should begin studying for finals starting on the first day of classes in August.

It is a MUST that you attend all your classes and actively take notes. Additionally, when you get home each day, it is IMPERATIVE that you review your notes for each class. It has been scientifically proven that students will remember concepts better when they start reviewing them at an earlier period of time before a test. When reviewing each concept, make note of things that you are having trouble grasping and seek the help of your teachers after school. It is better to ask for your teachers' help early in the semester, rather than the week before a final, as there is the possibility that there may be many students seeking help the week of exams.

During the week leading up to the exam, you should be fairly well prepared for your finals. The key to preparing well the week before is to continually review your material that you have learned. With subjects like Math and Chemistry, it is important to not only understand the material, but also to complete many practice problems.

With subjects like English and History, the most important thing is to comprehend all the readings that have been assigned to you. I know that History and English can have many difficult terms that are hard to understand, so it is important to take your time, as opposed to just skimming through them.

On the day of the final that you are taking, I recommend not attempting to continue cramming things into your brain. If you have been correctly studying ahead of time, you should be very well prepared for the test, and making yourself anxious by trying to find concepts that you still don't understand may actually hurt you on the test. The most important thing to have when you walk into the testing room is confidence. If you have a positive attitude when taking the test, your brain will work much more efficiently and not be bogged down by stress or anxiety.

HOW TO PREPARE FOR FINALS

- Start studying the first day of class

- Ask a teacher for help if you are having trouble with a concept

- Do practice problems

- Understand all readings

- Go to the test with confidence

- Math/Science: create formula pages

- Language: vocabulary, pages for practicing verbs tenses

- English/History: remember the important people, dates, concepts, etc.

- Write a 4-week schedule prior to the final to re-review all concepts

- Re-read the November – 9th Grade chapter, as studying for midterms is similar to finals

10TH GRADE

HOW TO KEEP UP THE MOMENTUM: PSAT

As hard as it can be to leave summer and crack down on work again, it's always exciting to start up another school year. New classes, new teachers, and new friends make everything a little bit more exciting at the start of the year. Usually there's a bit of a lull in tests and major assignments, because your teachers want to give you the time to adjust to your new schedule and prepare to work hard again. While it may be tempting to spend your free time with friends, going to the movies, or whatever else teenagers do these days, September provides the perfect opportunity for you to pay some attention to something really important outside of your classes: the PSAT.

First, don't stress yourself out just yet. I know it is overwhelming and feels too early for test prep, but this can do you a lot of favors in the future. This test won't actually affect you very much until you take it as a junior, so sit back, relax, and use this as a practice round to get a feel for what the PSAT is like, and to learn what you need to work on before the real deal next year. The test is usually offered in October, so you'll have around a month to prepare yourself or get an academic coach.

So what is the PSAT? It's a test with questions similar to those you'll find on the SAT, but it is much shorter and does not include any writing component. It will contain questions based on your comprehension of reading, language, and math. All of the questions are multiple choice, and the graders deduct a fraction of points for each wrong answer. You will receive a score out of 240.

Also similar to the SAT, preparation for this test is the key to getting a good score. There are numerous prep books and classes available to accommodate a wide variety of price ranges. Pick whichever study strategy works best for you and your learning style. Some people really could use the extra accountability of a coach in order to stay on top of their studies and make sure they don't fall behind. Coaches also have the benefit of providing a resource to whom you can ask questions, and from whom you can get personalized help on the sections that challenge you the most. You should decide how much time to commit to studying each day, and you can speed up or slow down to focus only on the sections in which you need improvement. Start in September at the very latest to prepare for the test, using whichever learning approach best suits your academic needs.

Okay, so you know what to do and when to do it in order to achieve your best possible PSAT score. But why is it so important? Colleges won't see your PSAT score on your applications, and it won't have much effect on your high school career, outside of one major benefit: National Merit. The PSAT is also called the NMSQT, or the National Merit Scholarship Qualifying Test. Based on your score when you take the test as a junior, you may receive the opportunity to be commended or even receive a scholarship from the National Merit Scholarship Program. The scores required for each cutoff are based on state average scores, so they change each year and vary by state depending on how well students perform on that specific test.

First, of the over a million participants in the nation who take the test, the top 50,000 or so are selected based purely on their total PSAT scores. From these, the lower scores receive the first level of recognition. They are sent letters notifying them that they are "Commended Scholars." Commended scholars do not continue on in the competition, but they have a nice piece of recognition that they can write on their resumes or college applications.

The highest-scoring 16,000 students are recognized as National Merit Semi-Finalists. Everyone who is named a semi-finalist will get access to an application that they need to fill out in order to continue on in the competition. Using this application, around 15,000 of the semi-finalists receive the distinction of National Merit Finalist.

Being a National Merit Finalist will open up doors when the time comes to apply for college. Some schools offer scholarships to all National Merit Finalists that can range from a thousand a year, to huge scholarship packages that can include full rides, laptops, and all sorts of perks if you choose their school! Basically, earning the title of National Merit Scholar can pay for all of your college and then some, depending on the school that you choose. And even if your university of choice does not provide this kind of merit aid, the title is still a great honor to list on your resume and on all of your college applications.

TO SUMMARIZE

- Taking the PSAT can open some huge doors.

- Your score is not extremely important until your junior year, so RELAX and use this first round of the test as a practice round!

- Buy a book, get an academic coach, or do whatever you think will best prepare you for the test. Coaches can also be a great resource if you have extra questions on concepts that you still don't understand!

- Take the test in October and focus on the feedback they give you: which were your strongest and weakest sections? What do you need to work on the most? And what is a reasonable target score for the real deal, when you take the test as a junior?

- Take advantage of this lull at the beginning of the school year to really get on top of your PSAT studies, and you'll be more than fine by the time the test comes.

HOW TO MANAGE YOUR TIME WISELY

....

This skill is the biggest one. If you can master this, you can master anything. Guess what—you and Bill Gates have the SAME amount of time during the day to work. Nuts, eh? Here is a chart I do with many of my students to show them their time through the week. For many of them, it blows them away.

In One Week: (7 days * 24 hours = 168 hours)

Usually, this is what the chart looks like with a student who is not managing their time well in sports:

- School: 35 hours

- Sports: (including Games and practices): 18 hours

- Dinner: 9 hours

- Family Commitments: 3 hours

- Church: 3 hours

- Sleep: 49 hours

- Socializing (1 each day of the week + weekend sleepovers): 20 hours

- Jacking around on the computer: 7 hours

- Getting ready / Showering: 7 hours

- Homework: 17 hours

TOTAL: 151 hours

17 hours on homework for roughly each class = 3.5 hours per week per subject, which is roughly only 40 minutes on the school week to spend per class. Guess what, 40 minutes per class is nothing compared to what you need to be doing to get A's in class, especially prepping for tests and quizzes.

Usually, this is what the chart looks like with a student who is managing their time with a balanced life:

- School: 35 hours

- Sports: (including Games and practices): 18 hours

- Dinner: 7 hours

- Family Commitments: 3 hours

- Church: 3 hours

- Sleep: 52.5 hours

- Socializing: 6 hours

- Jacking around on the computer: 3 hours

- Getting ready / Showering: 7 hours

- Homework: 33.5 hours

TOTAL: 134.5 hours

You get more sleep on this plan, and you are ready to really study for classes. You can study roughly 6.7 hours per week for each class – which means you are really getting in a good amount of time to prepare for each class, whether it is outline notes, re-reading chapters, going over test preparation, or making note cards. This is a good amount of time to really succeed in a class. Sleep is so important, and I have always slept a minimum of 7.5, upwards of 8 hours each night – even until now. When I sleep less than 7, I am a mean, grumpy machine.

If you do not do sports, you are given an extra 18 hours per week – which is an extra 3.6 hours per class each week, which is a great amount of time. Unfortunately, a lot of students that do not play sports, tend to add up a lot of time watching TV, or jacking around on their computer. This means that in the balanced plan you get 33.5 hours per week, and 51.5 hours on the second plan. I can tell you that if you are taking all Honors and AP classes, not doing sports can make you feel less overwhelmed, exhausted, or pulled in too many directions. Challenging classes require time-intensive homework and preparation, which can leave many athletes feeling stressed – or literally brain dead.

HOW TO HANDLE EXTRACURRICULAR ACTIVITIES

....

This is a hot button topic people. Let me tell you why. I get calls all the time from parents who are wondering why their student is suffering academically when they are doing the following: two sports, one or two organizations on campus, church events, family stuff, and somehow having friends. People, are you kidding me? This is like telling me that I have 50 hours in the day. I will admit, I was not ever good at sports, and it honestly has a lot to do with the gene pool of being Indian. Academics is our sport, and we are literally Gold medalists. So, every time I tried to do a sport, not only was it a blow to my self-esteem, but it was also such a time-eater. I was a bench lover in soccer, volleyball, and basketball. How many hours a day were taken for me to run around, sweat, feel like crap, and then lose 2 hours between 4 and 10 p.m. after being in five honors courses?

I distinctly remember this one time I joined the soccer team my sophomore year, and I was in Honors Chemistry with Mrs. R. My dad is a graduate of IIT, the NUMBER ONE college in the WORLD, and especially for chemical engineering (which, guys, it's harder than Harvard by a long shot). I came home and was on my bed, trying to understand chemical reactions. I literally remember being so exhausted from the soccer, that I looked down at my book while tears rolled down my face and hit the textbook, one after another, after another. I was so embarrassed that I was the daughter of a top engineer who moved to the States with only 20 bucks in his pocket and landed a job in Houston, Texas, at DuPont, and I couldn't understand chemical reactions.

What I didn't realize is that I had limitations on my energy levels, and my ability to focus and succeed in school. It is okay if you can't do it all. I tried to convince my dad to just tell me exactly how to do it, but with his levels of morals and ethics, he expected me to somehow translate this Chemistry textbook, which might have been written in Japanese for all I could tell, and I looked at him blankly. Exhausted, stuffed from eating too much at dinner since I had this amazing metabolism, and lying on my bed, all I wanted to do was sleep. I could care less about Chemistry, and to this day, I feel the same way because of how hard it was to balance both a sport like soccer, and a sport like Honors Chemistry. So, picking your extracurriculars wisely is extremely important.

Since I was starting to see my A's slip to A- and B+, I immediately dropped soccer—and trust me, NO one missed me. All I got was a Best Dressed Award, which by the way helped later, since I worked in fashion in NYC and had my own clothing line that sold in Whole Foods Body sections across the U.S. But at the time of high school, honestly it was smart for me to drop out of sports. Look, I don't recommend this for everyone, because there are so many students I have worked with who rock at sports. I mean seriously, like top soccer players who get automatic admission into college, or students who have such an amazing passion for running, it's almost—just almost—contagious (except I suck at running).

Here is my little recipe for what I think is good for extracurriculars. Find something you are passionate about. Do not join 10 activities, join 3 or 4 that matter to you. For me, I was intrigued by diversity, art, world relations, and community service. So I joined Diversity in Action, Students of Service, National Arts Honors Society, and Model United Nations. Make sure you stick to these all four years. Do not join crap and just jump around for four years. Find out what is interesting by attending the first three meetings—yes, I said THREE. The first one is all a marketing spiel about how awesome they are. Attend the clubs fair, get all the flyers you can, and read about some of the cool projects they do and how you can get involved. Eventually you will lead one of these organizations, or a team or a project within it, so make sure you get in deep when you join one of these. Colleges look at your level of commitment to these organizations, what you did to make a difference and change them in any way, projects you took on, etc. I will go into depth on how I left a legacy at my high school based on my involvement on campus – because I was totally in love with getting involved and making a difference in this way. If you choose to do a sport, please remember that genetically I was not built to do sports, as I enviously watched all the 5'6" long-legged girls rock at field hockey, run a mile in half the time it took me, and had such amazing hand-eye coordination, it was unreal. Most of the time, coaches would ask me to just come back in while I was attempting to run the first three laps, and had been lapped by everyone, and was nowhere near done. To someone who was at the top of their game academically, and then brutally embarrassed sports-wise, I decided to FOCUS on my strengths. But if you do a sport, I recommend one a semester. Don't try to do two sports. It is extremely difficult. You may not realize this, but being in school does require energy, focus, and mental attention – which is a sport in itself. So, don't make your schedule that you come home at 8 p.m. It will be nearly impossible. There was this one girl named Jane who was in the top of our class, who did it all. And I mean, did it ALL. Like sports, top honors classes, was written up in newspapers about her sports skills, etc. I personally don't think she slept. She was also super nice, so I kinda think she was a superhuman alien or something. Just remember these people are ANOMALIES.

HOW TO TACKLE PROCRASTINATION

....

It's the end of your first semester of 10th grade! You've done it...almost! You've got one more thing to overcome before you're officially done, and unfortunately it's what every student dreads the most—midterms. You've heard the horror stories before. All-nighters, hours of studying. And of course, the coffee. So much coffee. Fortunately for you, only one of these things has to be true (and no, it's not coffee), and that's studying. Don't be intimidated by the idea of midterms and by the horror stories that you may have heard. Everyone gets through them, and with the right planning and strategies, you will get through them much more easily than if you are totally unprepared.

First things first. You will have to study. There's no strategy for surviving midterms that doesn't involve studying, and there's no way around it. The key is to study correctly and efficiently. Spending your study hours actually studying will help you do much better on your exams. Seems like common sense, right? But for some reason, when a lot of students study they waste TONS of time, either on their laptops, texting, or simply not focusing. Get rid of the distractions and focus on what you're doing, and you'll have a much easier time and be much less stressed.

There are so many different studying methods, and everyone is different, so no one method is right for all. However, many strategies have been shown to be helpful to the majority of students, so try to employ as many of them as you can. The first rule is an obvious one. Everyone knows it, and it is by far the most important, but unfortunately it's the most ignored: Don't procrastinate!

This one's a tough one. Of course you would rather go and hang out with your friends, or watch your favorite show, or play your video game, than study for your midterms. What is it about students that makes them procrastinate? One of the most satisfying feelings in the world is finishing something early—it can be anything, a school assignment, a project, building something, a long-term goal you've set—because it means you've worked harder than you even planned to. You know what's not as satisfying? Finishing said assignment at 5 a.m. the night before it's due and knowing you have to be awake in 2 hours to go to school.

Not procrastinating is such an easy concept in theory, but so much harder for students in practice. Do your best to avoid it, and your midterm period will be infinitely easier. Don't wait to study your classes. You have much more challenging coursework this year! You have about a week or two to review everything you've learned in 5 months. You won't be able to do it in one night, and I promise you that if you try, you won't succeed, and you'll be miserable while you attempt it. Start studying as early as you can.

This brings me to the next topic: review sheets. These are your best friend, so treat them like gold! You wouldn't put off hanging out with your best friend until the last minute. Don't put off doing your review sheets. Begin filling them out as soon as your teachers give them to you. They tell you exactly what you need to study, and many of them are a good indicator of what the questions on the midterm will be. Filling out review sheets is also an excellent way to study, because it forces you to try and recall the information—and if you don't, to look it up in your notes or textbook. You get out as much as you put into them, so take the time to put in your best effort. If you fill them out thoroughly and completely, they will become excellent study tools, and in many cases one of the only study materials you will need (use your notes and textbook to brush up on topics that aren't included in the review, just in case).

Be sure to pay attention during class, especially during the days leading up to your midterm. Teachers more often than not will go over the review sheet, do reviews of their own, or answer questions. Getting studying done at school just means less you'll have to do by yourself at home, so why not take advantage of it? With your review sheets, try your best to handwrite them. As someone who types much, much faster than I can write, I know how tedious handwriting things can be. However, all research points to the fact that you remember better when you write it down, as opposed to just saying it or typing it. You've probably seen this already in your school work. If you start early on the reviews, you'll have a lot of extra time, and handwriting the review sheets means you will remember more of the information, which you won't have to study as much later.

As far as the best ways to study, review sheets are definitely the dominant method. Don't rely solely on them, though. Teachers won't put everything on the review sheet, or they may put a topic where a question could pop up that's similar, but not quite exactly what you put down on your review sheet. So be sure to use other sources when studying. Go back and review your notes. For especially difficult concepts, crack open your textbook and read the chapter on it. For some reason, some teachers don't emphasize using a textbook, or students don't utilize them effectively when in school. Knowing how to read, study, and learn from a textbook is an extremely important skill to have, as it will be your primary source of learning when you get to college. So start now and learn how to use it.

If you are studying for math, or a science that requires problem-solving such as chemistry, physics, or economics, do problems! This is so important. Re-reading your notes from the semester will not be enough. Make formula cheat sheets for every chapter. You need to learn how to approach problems, and the only way to do that is to work them out until you can do them with your eyes closed. The more problems you do, the better off you will be.

Along with avoiding procrastination is how to space your studying. A lot of students cram (mostly as a result of procrastination. If you don't procrastinate, you shouldn't have to cram). Cramming is by far the worst form of studying. Trying to learn a lot of material in a short amount of time is not going to work. Some of you may think you are good at cramming. I promise you that you will be even better if you space out your studying and start earlier. The best form of studying is distributed over several days, learning a little bit each day, and going back to review what you've studied every day to make sure you don't forget anything. Students who study like this are much more likely to remember information than those who cram.

Problem is, you don't have time to study days for a class and do that for 5 or 6 classes. So what do you do? Study for multiple tests during the same time period. Spend an hour studying for math, take a break, and then an hour studying for history. Studies show that studying a different topic doesn't interfere with your learning, so if you study for history after math, you won't forget what you just learned. Studying for another subject is like giving your brain a break from studying the previous subject, but be sure to take breaks from studying altogether as well.

Take breaks. I can't stress this enough. A lot of students seem to forget this when it comes to midterms, because they are stressed and panicking and feel like they can't stop studying. Contrary to what you may believe, there is such a thing as overworking. If you are too tired, you will not work nearly as efficiently, your productivity will decrease, and you'll get less out of your studying time. And I mean real studying, like rigorously filling out your review sheet, constantly doing problems, or trying to memorize information. Then go and walk around your house. Get a snack, or play with your dog. Then come back and continue studying.

Try not to let your five-minute breaks become hours long. I recommend you don't go and watch TV for five minutes, because chances are you'll waste much more time than that. Limit your Internet exposure while you study, too. If possible, don't have a computer in front of you when you are studying. Resist the temptation to do anything on it besides your work (like going on Buzzfeed—you'll spend hours clicking related articles).

Exercise - yes, get some exercise. It doesn't really matter what it is. It doesn't have to be some crazy workout like Cross Fit (although if you want to do it, more power to you!). Just go outside and move! Ride a bike or go on a run. Play a sport with your friends (a great way to spend time with your friends without using them as an excuse to procrastinate). Go lift at the gym. Do yoga! I can't tell you how relaxing yoga can be, and how helpful it can be in clearing your mind and rejuvenating your body. (Yes, even guys can do yoga. It's just as important as lifting weights or cardio, and in some cases, better.).

Exercise is amazing in so many ways. First, it gives you a break from studying and takes your mind off it for a little bit. It also does so in a way that doesn't involve watching TV or going on the Internet and filling your brain with useless information that gets in the way of your studying. Second, it gets your blood pumping to everywhere in your body, most importantly to your brain. Remember, you're sitting down at a desk for most of the day at school and when you study, and for many of you, while you're watching TV on a couch. Make sure to be active to keep blood circulating properly and everything working perfectly. Exercise also releases endorphins in your body, like serotonin and dopamine, which are associated with feelings of happiness. Equally important, if not more important, than you getting good grades on your midterms is you being happy. Don't let school get in the way of your mental and physical health. Lastly, exercise helps you sleep better at night, making you more energized during the day. Who doesn't love sleeping better?

Speaking of energy, no discussion of midterms is complete without talking about the one thing you've probably heard the most about - coffee. Contrary to what you may have heard, coffee is definitely not necessary! You're only a sophomore. It's a little too early to be drinking large amounts of coffee, if you ask me. Give it a few more years, if ever. Even as a college student, I still don't drink coffee because I don't like the taste. It's definitely not required.

Nothing beats sleep, and no amount of coffee or Red Bull or 5 Hour Energy will compensate for the lack of a good night's rest. If you plan right, all-nighters are completely unnecessary, and are actually detrimental to both your health and your studying. Just start early, and make sure you get a good amount of sleep every night.

The last point that I want to emphasize is to remain calm. Don't panic about your first midterms. Just remember to use all the strategies and "rules" above, and you will breeze right through them. Develop good study habits for midterms now, because you'll be having final exams all throughout your education, and the earlier you start, the easier it is for you. I'll finish up with some Do's and Don'ts that summarize the list of strategies for midterms that will help you finish the semester strong.

Do's and Don'ts for Midterms

DO

- Start early. The earlier you start, the easier it is and the less stressed you'll be. Some schools have their first semester finals after the Christmas break. If this is you, take advantage of that! Start studying over the vacation, even if it's only for a little bit.

- Practice as many problems as you can. This is most important for math. Practice, practice, practice! You've heard the saying practice makes perfect. As cliché as it is, it is true.

- Remain healthy. Exercise. GET PLENTY OF SLEEP. Not only will you study better, but you'll get sick less. There's nothing worse than being sick during your finals. Except pulling an all-nighter to study while you're sick.

- Relax afterwards. Celebrate the fact that you finished your first semester of 10th grade and (hopefully) aced your midterms. Take some time to unwind. You definitely earned it!

DON'T

- Procrastinate. I've said it so many times, and yet everyone still has a tendency to do it. Fight the urge! You'll thank yourself for not putting off your work when you are done studying, and everyone else is panicking and studying last-minute.

- Stress too much. A little bit of stress is normal, of course, but don't let yourself be overwhelmed.

- Worry if you don't do as well as you had hoped. Especially don't let it get to your head. You have other exams, so push it out of your mind and focus on the present. What's done is done, and it's out of your control.

HOW TO RE-EVALUATE YOUR GOALS

···

Last year at this time, we talked about making goals. This year, as a sophomore, you have a bit of experience under your belt. This New Year, use your old goals as a springboard for this year's goals. To start, look back. What goals did you set? How successful were they? Taking time to reflect on your goals of last year can help you decide what goals you need to set this year. By reevaluating old goals, you can edit them to fit any changes you made in your life.

As a sophomore, you should still be focused on shaping your high school experience. You are still under halfway done with high school, so you have plenty of time to think about colleges and majors and life post-high school, but now is the time to focus on your goals regarding your personal interests.

Now, you have the time to try out new things, such as arts, computer programming, math clubs, or a new language. Figuring out what you like now will be very helpful when you need to start making decisions about where you want to go to college. Set your goals academically, but also keep your interests in mind. Find a goal that focuses on expanding your horizons and trying new things. As an underclassman, you have the time and the resources to explore. Put an incentive behind it. Tell yourself that you will try three new things, and do them! Evaluate your experiences, keep a journal, and focus on how successful you were, and in particular how the event made you feel. Did you find volunteering extremely fulfilling? What about a particular sport?

One thing to keep in mind is that achieving success and fulfillment are both important goals. How fulfilled are you? What goals do you have that are focused on taking care of yourself? Some goals I like to have are: build a morning routine, think about 3 things I'm thankful for, and take 2 minutes to be silent in the morning.

Additionally, you should keep up good goal-making habits. Set ambitious goals, but think carefully about what you think that you can achieve. Also, remember that these are your goals—not your parents' goals, not your teachers' goals, or anyone else's. You can't borrow ambition from someone else. You have to find it within yourself to achieve your goals. Make sure to evaluate all parts of your life: academic health, spiritual and relationships. Keep tracks of all areas in your life.

HOW TO GET LEADERSHIP ROLES

··

Throughout your freshman year in high school, it's easy to come up with excuses and avoid joining organizations. You're still adjusting, you have a harder workload, you don't know which clubs are available, and you haven't discovered what you're interested in. During your freshman year, these are all valid. You don't want to over-commit or accidentally join a club that you're not interested in. However, if you let this attitude continue through the rest of your underclassman years, then you'll miss out on the chance to impress colleges with your leadership abilities, and find organizations that spark your passion.

Hopefully, during your freshman year, you had the chance to start thinking about joining a few clubs - student council, chess club, environmental club, or whatever may interest you. Hopefully, at the beginning of your sophomore year, your interests were so peaked that you joined one or two clubs.

If this isn't you, don't worry—it isn't too late. Shoot to join at least one club before the end of your sophomore year, though. You might be thinking, "How in the world am I supposed to find out about these clubs?!" The easiest ways are:

- Make friends with some of your teachers. They might be the teacher in charge of a club that interests you!

- Meet some juniors or seniors. They know all of the clubs and would be happy to tell you what some of them are.

- Be on the lookout for an organization fair that your school might put on. Usually these consist of booths for each club, so that you can walk up and hear what they're all about.

Why is it so important to get involved early on? Well, it's important to become involved in something so that you can expand your interests, become more well-rounded, and gain knowledge that you might not acquire in the classroom. Sometimes, it's important to join clubs so you can meet friends that you wouldn't encounter otherwise. Other times, it's just good to have a place to de-stress and not focus on just academics.

One of the most important reasons to get involved early, is to make your presence known to other members of the group. Come junior and senior year, it's going to be important to exercise and develop your leadership skills—but how are you going to get elected president, vice president, or secretary if no one in the clubs knows who you are? You're not. That's the bottom line.

Now you might be thinking it's not that big of a deal if you don't have any leadership experience. This is one of the biggest misconceptions that high school students have today. Admissions boards at colleges think that being involved in a leadership roles shows you are mature, can hold the respect of your classmates, and care about something enough to become that involved.

IN SUMMARY

- Get involved early, but be careful and only get involved with things you're interested in.

- Just clicking a box to join a club isn't good enough. You have to make your presence known and be active.

- By this point in your sophomore year, you should be thinking about running for a leadership position.

- Leadership shows colleges that you're mature, respected, and engaged.

HOW TO EXPLORE SUMMER OPPORTUNITIES

....

At this point in time, I bet there are two thoughts going through your head: 1. How many days until summer?... and 2. I can't wait to sit around and sleep for three months. The first thought is a good one (staying on top of things and preparing for the summer to come, not the fact that you are dreading school and want it to end), but the second needs to be eliminated as soon as possible.

Imagine yourself sitting in a college admission interview in just a year and half. Undoubtedly, they are going to ask how you utilized your summers. If your only response is that you caught up on sleep and worked on your suntan, do you really think colleges will be impressed? The answer is a big, fat NO.

I'm sure you're wondering, though, what kinds of things you can get involved in during the summers at your age. Many of you are not 16 yet and cannot hold many jobs, but if making money is appealing to you, then search some out! There are plenty of summer camps looking for counselors, local pools looking for water safety instructors and lifeguards, and people in your neighborhoods looking for help around the yard and house. Having a job after your sophomore year shows that you are mature in thinking about money, that you aren't lazy, and that you have a good work ethic.

If making money and having a job doesn't sound very appealing to you, or if you might want something a little more low-key than a full-time job, you can always explore research opportunities. Many local hospitals or universities partner with high school students to provide 2 to 3 week research opportunities to spark interest in young minds. If you're interested in basic sciences or engineering, this is totally for you!

For all of you out there who think you want to be a doctor, summers are a great time to reach out to local physicians and ask about shadowing. Be realistic when you are asking them to take time out of their day to babysit you, and only ask for maybe a week or two of their time. However, that doesn't mean you can only ask one doctor. Pick a few different specialties and see what different branches of medicine are all about. This shows extreme interest and maturity for colleges, too!

Again, if none of these sound interesting to you, just figure out something that does. If volunteering is your thing, then partner with a local organization and work 15 hours or so a week to help them out. You can even pick more than one organization. If you're a dedicated athlete, pour yourself into your sport to show colleges your dedication. If you are a computer nerd, take the summer to teach yourself a new coding language. Just make sure what you're doing is useful! The internet is full of opportunities, and many counselors at your school can also help you to get in the right direction.

HOW TO SET UP TEST PREP FOR THE SUMMER

··

When you start mapping out your summer and all of the cool jobs, volunteering, research, and shadowing that you'll have the chance to do, don't forget to consider standardized test preparation. All year you are studying and preparing for things like tests and finals during school, you get caught up in the fun happenings of summer and completely forget about preparing for the PSAT, SAT, and ACT.

There's a nasty rumor that has been going around high schools across America for years: there's nothing you can do to prepare for the PSAT, SAT, or ACT. Don't listen to this. If you can't walk into your first practice test and make a perfect score, then there are obviously things you can do to prepare.

The first and most important step to test preparation is taking a diagnostic test. Who knows, you might get a perfect score the first time and really not need any sort of formal test preparation - but do you really want to take the chance of walking in on test day, not knowing your current base score? Taking a diagnostic test can help you figure out exactly which sections you need to focus on, how much time you need to devote to studying, and can give you a general idea of what the test will be like on the big day.

Aside from actually telling you what you know and what you need to work on, test preparation can help to ease your nerves on test day. If you've never seen what the PSAT looks like and you walk into the test room cold turkey, you're going to be nervous. If you've seen fifteen or twenty practice tests, know exactly how much time to spend on each problem, and feel confident in your mastery of the material, you'll walk in on test day with much more peace of mind, and in a better overall mental state.

We offer our students test prep packages to help with every section of the test. We have helped students over and over to get the scores of their dreams!

SO WHY IS TEST PREP SO IMPORTANT?

- Taking a diagnostic test at home can help you figure out exactly what to study

- Diagnostic tests can also help you figure out how much you need to study

- You'll be less nervous and feel more prepared on test day

- These tests impact college admission and how much money you get!

11TH GRADE

11TH GRADE

HOW TO UNDERSTAND THE SAT

· ·

Three letters have never been more daunting than S.A.T. It literally spells sat. Why can't it just mean Saturday? I love Saturdays. That is the general sentiment high school students have toward the SAT. I will be very forward with you. The only way to increase your score is to know your weaknesses and study from practice tests. You can be great at English and Math in high school, but if you are unfamiliar with the format of the test and the questions, then you will not do as well as you could have.

So let's break down these three scary letters and make it relatively easy.

The next step is to buy some practice workbooks, and if you do not have access to those, there are plenty of practice tests online at collegeboard.com. I will say it again: The best way to improve your score is to work through practice tests. The more you familiarize yourself with the format, the easier it will be.

SPEAKING OF FORMAT, HERE IS A BREAKDOWN OF THE SAT

- It takes 3 hours and 45 minutes

- There are a total of 10 sections with three subjects (Reading, Writing, Math)

- Math = Algebra, Geometry, and Pre-calculus

- Writing = Grammar + Essay

- Reading = vocabulary, reading comprehension

- The test costs $51 (do not worry if you cannot come up with the money, there are waivers online that allows you to pay a lower fee)

- The highest score possible is 2400. Each section is worth 800 points.

- Sign up for available tests on the college board website. You can pick the dates and times that you are available.

- Send your scores in through college board to the colleges you are applying to (there is also a fee, but it can be waived as well).

You probably stopped reading the list halfway down. I know, I'm sorry I couldn't make this more interesting, but they are the facts! If you know how to tackle the SAT, you will have an easier time studying for it.

A lot of people do not realize there is help out there. There are many tutoring companies that specialize in SAT prep, and high school tutors such as Elite Private Tutors, my company. The SAT is not designed to make you fail; it is designed to test you on what you have learned throughout high school. IT IS DESIGNED TO TEST

WHAT YOU HAVE LEARNED IN HIGH SCHOOL. So, what have you learned in high school?

Most people will say nothing, or at least nothing practical. I felt the same way too. I don't need to know how fast two trains are coming at each other in real life. All I need to know is that I'm out of the way so I don't die. But the reality is, high school helps. High school is USEFUL, despite what all your friends might say. I realized this at the end of my junior year. I had already taken the SAT once after going to SAT boot camps, and yet I could not get the score I wanted. It was not until I took it again during my junior year that I got the score I wanted. Of course the tutoring helped, and if you have the opportunity to sign up for a tutor, take it! But the biggest thing that helped me was my junior year English teacher. He would give us weekly lists of vocabulary words and constantly test us on reading comprehension, until English became my best subject. Keep in mind, you can do thus sophomore year with a coach or a test prep book.

HERE ARE SOME TIPS TO IMPROVE ON EACH SECTION

- Writing: LEARN THE RULES FOR GRAMMAR. If you know the rules, the answers just pop out at you.

- Math: Do practice problems. But don't just do them. Understand why you got something wrong, so you can improve.

- Reading: This one is simple. READ. Read a lot. It will increase your reading speed. If you have time, I would recommend reading leisure books and keeping a journal of what you read for the day. This helps you improve on reading comprehension, and it is fun!

On March 5, 2014, the College Board announced that a redesigned version of the SAT would be administered for the first time in 2016. The exam will revert to the 1600-point scale, the essay will be optional, and students will have 3 hours to take the exam plus 50 additional minutes to complete the essay.

HOW TO BUID RELATIONSHIP WITH TEACHERS

....

In high school, it's easy to forget about building relationships with your teachers. We're often more concerned with making friendships with our peers, so we never think of bonding with a teacher. It's not about "brown nosing," it's about genuinely taking an interest in what they are trying to teach you as a person. When I was in my 10th grade year of high school, I had a biology teacher who loved to play reggae music. I shared the same love. One day I decided to comment on the songs she would play, and tell her how much I enjoyed it. It led to a great discussion of music and science, and her teaching me some great life lessons.

We often forget that our teachers are people too. We look at them as someone who instructs us to do our homework, or teaches us the fundamentals of certain courses. We don't realize that they go home and listen to their favorite songs the same way you and I do. It's very important to build a relationship with your teachers. It opens you up to a greater learning experience. You end up feeling more comfortable with asking questions in class, or just sitting and discussing a lesson you found interesting.

For some people building a relationship may come easy, and for others it may not. I always say there are three simple steps you should follow to help gain that relationship.

FIRST STEP TO BUILDING A RELATIONSHIP

- Find something you have in common.

- If you are unable to find something you have in common, take notice of something you feel they really enjoy.

- Bring an article related to the subject they teach and talk about your opinion.

SECOND STEP

- Don't be afraid to ask questions.

- If you have a teacher who gives you short answers, that's okay. Continue to state that you would like a more in-depth answer. Let them know you genuinely care about what they are teaching.

- Ask for their advice.

THIRD STEP

- Show motivation. The more motivated you appear, the more noticed you will get.

- Not only will it help with your relationship building, but it will also help you in subjects you are having trouble with.

WHAT IS THE PRACTICAL USE OF BEFRIENDING TEACHERS

- Can provide insight into the college application process and college experience.

- Can provide general mentorship.

- Can write a letter of recommendation - BINGO!

HOW TO ANALIZE PROGRESS REPORTS AND GPA CALCULATOR

....

Ooh, the dreaded progress reports. What I love is that so many parents aren't getting progress reports anymore, so kids are getting away with murder. And then, of course, I tell them that they can log in to the school website from the parents' side and see it, and then the students are like oh, crapola. Anyway, progress reports are not supposed to be some horrible experience, people. It's like getting your blood work from your doc and finding out you have to eat better. It helps you to tactically and strategically make some shifts if you didn't follow our study tips, and figure out how to re-apply them.

Let's analyze a progress report. Depending on whether your school does a halfway one, or three per semester, it is a good way for you to figure out what you need to be better. Guess what—in college you don't even get one of these, so you have NO idea how you are doing. Then again, you only take like two tests and a final in a college course, so basically you only have a few grades to make a difference, compared to high school where you get some crazy mini-quiz every week to just boost your grade for fun. The report tells you exactly what your grade is at that time, based upon all prior work. So, if you are in History and making a B, it means that you have made some C's and some A's, or just straight-up all B's until that point.

YOU NEED TO FIGURE OUT THE FOLLOWING

- How do I keep my grades A's instead of C's, and why are my grades fluctuating so much in this class?

- Or, why am I only making B's every time? What am I doing that I could be doing better? What does it take to make an A in this class? Are there key concepts I am missing, or a better way I should be taking my notes? Ask your teacher!

Here is an example formula for understanding your grades.

History

- 25% homework

- 50% tests

- 25% participation

Let's say it's 95 for homework, 80 for tests and 70 for participation. Then you would multiply 95 by 0.25 + 80 by 0.50 and 70 by 0.25. This gives you 23.75 + 40 + 17.5 = 81.25%

This formula shows you exactly what you need to know about what your grades mean.

These are amazing questions to ask your teacher in private – so that they know you are taking the initiative to improve. Take notes based on your conversation, and use them to reset your semester.

Also, this is a great time to hire a tutor if you haven't done so. Usually we come in and what takes you three hours, we get done in an hour, tops. Holes or gaps in what you have learned can affect the rest of your semester, especially if it is cumulative like a language or math class – and you DO not want to continually miss points because of something from August.

HOW TO APPLY TO MEDICAL FOCUSED PROGRAMS FOR COLLEGE

....

I want to tell you about the process of going into medical school: what you do during high school, what to do in college, and what comes afterwards.

STEPS FOR GETTING INTO MED SCHOOL

1. Undergraduate or Bachelors Degree (four years of college)

2. Make having a high GPA your #1 priority

3. Be active in extracurricular activities (related to medicine preferred)

4. Have good relationships with your professors

5. Take and pass the MCAT exam

WHAT CAN YOU DO IF YOU ARE STILL IN HIGH SCHOOL?

- Start researching Science and Premedical programs for college

- Join any health-related clubs

- Volunteer at a hospital or clinic, or rotate with a doctor

- Get involved with Science Fair or other competitions

Start researching Premedical programs that accept you during high school. Historically, medical schools have been known to only accept students who have done a science major (biology, chemistry, physics). This is not the case anymore, BUT it still helps you a lot.

Think about it this way. Medical school is four years long. The first two years will be spent mostly in class, and the third and fourth years are the fun ones where you spend all day in the hospital, learning and treating patients. Science subjects are the foundations of the courses you will take those four years. It is true that medical schools want more diversity in their students, and they will happily accept arts, business, and humanities majors. But the reality is that if you don't do a science major, it will be more challenging to get into one.

So why is a science major so important? The first two years of med school are the most challenging. All the subjects have similar foundations. What do I mean by this? Science! For example, Pharmacology is used to understand medicine, Microbiology is used to understand how infections happen, and Physiology is used to learn how the body works. Basically, you have to know the normal way everything in the body occurs first, before you can learn how it works incorrectly (a disease). So it's of great help if you know Biology, Chemistry and Physics before you enter med school. It's been proven that students who don't do a science major during college struggle more during medical school.

Put yourself in the Dean's position: would you want a student who quickly understands the subjects, or one who will struggle because he/she has to learn everything for the first time? The answer is obvious. What I want to tell you is this: Choose the major which you are more passionate about, the one you love. If it's a science major, EVEN BETTER! Your chances of getting into medical school after college are even greater. What's best of all is having a premedical major!

Premedical Majors

Most colleges and universities have programs that are designed to walk you through the process of going to medical school. They involve clinical experience, medical research, volunteer activities, and preparation for the MCAT—which is sort of like an SAT, but for medical school. So if you have decided that you want to be a doctor or veterinarian, or get into pharmacology, this is the path to go! It is like following the yellow brick road right into medical school.

Then what?

All medical schools in the country have their own selection for new students, but they are all very similar.

Basic requirements

• MCAT EXAM

• College GPA

• Volunteering, Clinical rotations, Premedical Internships

- Professor recommendation letters

- Filling out the online application

After you graduate from college or during your last year, you should take an exam called MCAT (Medical College Admission Test). Right now you are probably worried about the SAT, because it's the key to opening the doors for college. So don't worry about the MCAT yet. The MCAT consists of Biology, Chemistry, Physics, and Math. This is why I placed a strong emphasis on the importance of doing your college major in one of these. It will make your life a lot easier.

COLLEGE GPA

Try to rock on your BCPM grades! I'm sure you have never heard about this abbreviation before. It stands for "Biology, Chemistry, Physics, and Math." Medical schools know you can take a lot of easy courses during college... they are very sneaky! Even though they do look at your overall GPA, they mainly focus on these subjects. They average them and then obtain a BCPM GPA. There are multiple calculators online that can help you average it. But remember, this is only useful for your college transcript. So if you're in high school right now, it's awesome if you start improving in these subjects and really take them seriously in college.

VOLUNTEERING, CLINICAL ROTATIONS AND PREMEDICAL INTERNSHIPS

This is an area where it is easy and fun for you to shine! Call your local Planned Parenthood clinic, animal shelter, or any hospital to see if they need an extra free hand to help out. If you have any family or family friends who are physicians, have your family give them a call, or call them yourself. Tell them you are interested in learning and observing their field. Most doctors will tell you that they will gladly accept you into their practice to learn. This can be started while you're still in high school! Try to expose yourself as much as you can to your community, and to the medical field. When it's time for you to apply to a medical school, there is an online application, and there are 15 spaces dedicated to the internship or learning experience section for clinical rotations and volunteering you completed to show your commitment and passion to the field.

HOW TO STAY HEALTHY UNDER STRESS

If you want to be at your best, you need to feel your best. It's about staying active, eating right, and building mental strength. There are many ways you can do this without joining some of the sport teams in high school.

If you do decide to join the volleyball team, it's not about just showing up to practice. It is about trying to show an effort at improving yourself from the inside out. Many studies have proven that the more you exercise, the higher your serotonin levels become (your happy neurotransmitter). A happier you equals a better you.

IF YOU DECIDE TO GO THE SPORTS ROUTE, LEARN THIS

- Punctuality: This is valid for everything you'll do. Job interview, hairdresser appointment, or going to the movie theater to watch a movie.

- Team Spirit: Playing in a team allows you to learn roles, positions and communication. You'll also need this within the company you'll end up working for, as well as within your family life and with your significant other.

- Practicing sports also places you in a "win" mood: create your goals, and do the best you can to reach them.

- Socially, sports are great: you'll get to meet new people, and you will have to work with them to reach the same goal, together. And possibly enjoy a cool celebration when you achieve something great as a team!

- Discipline: sports involve rules that need to be followed.

- Competition: That's real life. You may not win all the time, and it's great to be prepared for this before you step into adult life.

- Loyalty: Great team players stay in the game and play their best—even when they are losing—defending their team name, city and honor!

- Finally, playing sports is also a way to balance and/or enhance school accomplishments. You may not have rocked your Math test today, but you won the soccer game!

WHAT YOU NEED TO DO TO GET YOURSELF ACTIVE AND FIT

• Make sure you are eating the right kind of food. It is a lot easier than it may seem. There are so many diet articles and health articles that it can become overwhelming. Well, it doesn't have to be. Check the ingredients of what you are eating. A good rule of thumb is if you can't understand the ingredient, it's probably not real food. Eat a well-rounded diet, and make sure to get some veggies, fruit, grains, and protein daily. This doesn't mean you have to cut out "junk food" all together - it's okay to have that bowl of midnight ice cream once in a while. It's when you have that bowl of ice cream every night that it becomes a bad habit! Try to limit your junk food or treat intake to only once a week. Plus, it will make those things taste better and be much more rewarding than before.

- As someone who has attended the number one health supportive culinary school in the world, I know that students are depleting their bodies of minerals, vitamins, and nutrition. It is vital that students regulate their blood sugar to help stop the "junk food" cravings. The number one problem I have with students is their inability to manage their focus and their moods. Food is a crucial part of why students are struggling with these two issues. I am going to be working on a cookbook focused on helping students with nutrition and their academic career, because I think many students succumb to peer pressure and eat junk instead of fueling their bodies. Remember to carry water with you to school, you really need to be drinking over 8 glasses a day. Also, carry nuts or healthy fruits (low in sugar) so that you can snack between classes. Many students skip breakfast, eat lunch around 11:30, eat junk food around 3:30, and then starve until dinner at 7:30. You should be eating almost every 2-3 hours, to keep your blood sugar steady. This way you won't be craving unhealthy foods, rather you will be taking ownership of your body, spirit, and mind.

- Hangry: I am the ultimate expression of hangry – a word developed that explains when you are hungry + angry. Every time that I don't eat on time or skip breakfast, I am literally a different person. Make sure you listen to your body and are in tune with how you are feeling throughout the day. Monitor your moods and stay hydrated.

- Top students know exactly what to eat to fuel their brain. Nuts, fruits, vegetables, and healthy foods keep their minds agile and able to focus during class and at home.

- Find an activity that you can enjoy. Exercising doesn't have to be work. Everyone is different. Some people enjoy a relaxing session of yoga, while others will enjoy a more fast-paced type of fitness. Find something that brings you joy!

- Mental fitness: One of the key ingredients of successful students is to practice calmness and manage anxiety. If you mentally prepare yourself for failure: you will fail.

HOW TO INCLUDE COLLEGE IN YOUR FUTURE

....

There are so many options that run through your mind while figuring out your path after high school. College helps you to grow as a person. The education you gain helps you to develop into a more well-rounded individual. The college degree you will receive helps to ensure your success in the future, and will result in a much higher salary!

From my experience in college, I never had more fun in my life. I made friends that I knew were going to last a lifetime. Even after the years have passed and we have graduated, we still manage to keep in touch. We discuss our successes, our new families, and the great times we had. Now, this isn't to seem like college is just one big party, because it's not. There is a plus side to a social life, but it's about experiencing new things that you really can't experience anywhere else.

I can still remember my first day of college. I walked into the classroom, nervous and unsure if I had made the right decision. I pulled out my brand new textbook and the materials needed for my first college class in English. The professor introduced himself as Mr. Banks. I knew my college experience was about to begin. Week after week I attended class, and every day I felt I was gaining a new perspective. College is the only time when you still have freedom, and are still allowed to fail, try new things and explore without real-world consequences.

College is so much more than just an education. It's about growing as an individual and maturing in ways you never thought you could. It is about finding your passion, changing the world, and making lifelong friends.

HOW TO HAVE FUN THROUGH ACTIVITIES YOU ENJOY

··

STOP. RIGHT NOW. Take a moment, look at your schedule, and ask yourself: are you having fun? Because if the answer is no, then you are going about high school in all the wrong ways.

Despite what all the teenage movies tell you, high school is not a hierarchy run by "the plastics," nor is it a place where uncool kids get bullied. Of course that stuff still happens, but I promise you this: if you are having fun in high school, you are doing it right.

First, let's define fun. Having fun doesn't mean playing on the playground. Having fun means getting involved in things that make you passionate and excited to work and be present every day. Having fun means feeling a type of stress that makes you want to work even harder, and strive to be even better. Having fun means getting involved in activities that bring you pure joy.

I can tell you right now that I had TONS of fun in high school. Sure, my classes were hard, and at times I felt like I had so much work I just wanted to crawl into my pillow fort, bury my body in layers of blankets, and watch Netflix all day. But I got myself into something that brought me so much joy and gave me a break from school, that I no longer needed to crawl into a hole and hide when things got hard. I played basketball.

If something went wrong at school, I played basketball. If something went wrong at home, I played basketball. If something went wrong with my friends, I played basketball. There is nothing more relaxing than feeling the muscles in my body work, the sweat pouring down my face, the sound of rubber sneakers on the floor, the swish of the ball falling through the net, the feel of the basketball sliding off my fingers as I rise to shoot. In that moment, my mind is blank. It is focused on one thing, and one thing only. Basketball.

Right now you are probably thinking that I'm crazy. WHO THE HECK THINKS RUNNING AND SWEATING IS FUN? My point is this. Everyone has something that makes him/her feel refreshed and motivated to tackle life again. Mine is basketball, but yours might be something different. You might find joy in debate, the chess club, cheerleading, student government, reading, playing video games, watching TV shows, cooking, spending time with yourself - the list goes on and never ends. Everyone has something that makes him/her feel refreshed and motivated to tackle life again.

The goal is to find YOUR THING early and start doing it. If you don't have a thing, that is perfectly fine. Join something, because it will not only increase the quality of your life, but also help you get into a top tier college.

Okay. I know. Now you must be thinking that I really am out of my mind. Something fun cannot possibly help me get into a better college. Getting into college is a serious process, and the letters f-u-n do not belong anywhere. But you see, here is the truth. YES, SOMETHING FUN CAN HELP YOU GET INTO COLLEGE.

Colleges like to see more than just your GPA and the SAT score. They want to see a person, a character, a student beyond the books. They want to see commitment, growth and maturity, and you can show all these things by getting involved in and excelling at something you love. For me, I joined the basketball team my freshmen year of high school, and worked hard and practiced until I made it onto the varsity team my sophomore year. I spent my entire sophomore year on the bench, and maybe touched the ball twice in a real game. I stuck with it and continued to work hard. Why? Because it brought me joy, gave me a break from studying, and was the one thing that I could do that didn't remind me of the pressures of succeeding in school.

My junior year, I started for the varsity team, and my senior year I became captain. I was able to write about my experience on my college application because I felt like my story showed how hard working, passionate, and persistent I was, and I felt like this would not be translated through just my grades and my test scores. I wanted colleges to see my ability to dedicate time to something I am passionate about, and my ability to show leadership through different avenues.

SUGGESTIONS

- Find your passion and go for it with fierce intensity

- It will give you an experience worth writing about, and it will be rewarding for your character

- It will be great for your quality of life as well

- It will make for a powerful college application, especially if you pick something extremely unique!

- Pick something that makes you want to get up every morning. If you want to save the whales, then save the whales - the world needs someone to do this!

HOW TO HANDLE FAFSA, FINANCIAL AID AND GET SCHOLARSHIPS

....

By the time you are a junior, you have taken many of the necessary steps toward making your post-graduation dreams a reality. By the time the acceptances start rolling in, you may find yourself worried about how you're going to pay for college. Trust me, this can be VERY stressful. I'm not here to tell you not to worry about it, but I do want to say: When it comes to paying for college, where there is a will, there is a way. Do you really, really want to go to college? Yes? Then there absolutely is a way to find the means to go.

When considering your options, often students and parents look to financial aid packages, but how do you even get to that step? For most colleges, there is a separate financial aid application that you fill out after submitting the application for admission. For the most part, this application will be for your parents to answer, so make sure to sit down with them when you get ready to fill it out. This can be stressful, so make sure to breathe during these hard conversations.

These applications can be scary and time-consuming, but they are absolutely necessary for receiving financial aid from the university – that means scholarships, grants, and loans. For many students, the biggest portion of the financial aid they receive comes from the university itself, so these applications are very important!

The second most important financial aid source is the federal government. If you're a junior in high school, you've probably heard of the FAFSA. It stands for the Free Application for Federal Student Aid, and it is very important. Many colleges look at this application when considering your financial aid package as well, so this form is doubly important. Aside from its use for your financial aid application, federal aid such as the Pell Grant is offered based on your FAFSA as well.

But wait! What if it's not enough? Sometimes you can get disappointing news on financial aid from the college you want to attend. If government aid and university aid are not enough, don't give up yet. There are still options! What organizations are you and your family a part of? Often churches, non-profit organizations, and clubs give out scholarships to graduating seniors each year. Exhaust all resources! These scholarships tend to be for less than ones from the universities, but they can certainly help with tuition, fees, room and board, or books. Go to your school's college counseling office to gain access to the applications for tons of scholarships.

These tend to be more specific, intended for students from certain backgrounds or those who have a specific intended major. Take the time to go through your school's list of scholarships carefully to see which ones you qualify for. APPLY FOR ALL OF THEM, even if you think it's a long shot. One thing I've learned, when it comes to scholarships, is that you'll never get the money that you don't apply for. Even scholarships for as little as $500 can make a difference. Trust me, it is worth the energy spent, the essays written, and the interviews given to make your college experience less financially stressful. Also, if you look at the Essay Prompts, you can use some content from your college application essays.

Understand that financial aid may play an important role in where you go to college—but at the end of the day, it should not be the most important factor. When it comes to paying for college, determination will help you succeed in attending your dream school. Trust me, there are SO MANY organizations, benefactors, and other resources that are looking for students like you to sponsor.

12TH GRADE

HOW TO MEET WITH YOUR COLLEGE COUNSELOR

Throughout the fall of your senior year, you will get bombarded with letters, emails, and brochures from colleges. While this can make you feel wanted and competitive as an applicant, it can also be overwhelming when trying to narrow down your choices. In August, colleges will start visiting your school to give you an opportunity to learn more about what they have to offer, and this can be a great time to get information that's important to you without having to look through mounds of online info or read through an entire brochure.

Colleges visits will typically have a short presentation prepared to show you the highlights of their school, but if you are interested in specific degree programs, extracurricular activities, or the social environment, the campus reps should be excellent resources for these things as well. These visits are an excellent opportunity to ask about details you couldn't find elsewhere, or just to get an overall sense of the school before applying.

While all of these exciting visits are happening, you should also be meeting with your college counselor. They will be able to provide tons of info about applications and timelines that it would take you forever to find on your own. In August, schedule a meeting with your counselor to talk about your options. If you give them your fields of interest and scores, they can often tell you which schools have the best programs and which ones you would fit in at.

It is important that you ask them to be honest with you about schools you can most likely get into, and which schools will be reachable schools for you. Although I'm sure you will be a great candidate (because you've been following the guidelines of this book), it is important to know the average scores and general student profiles of the schools, so that you understand your chances when applying.

After getting a list of possible schools from your counselor, it's time for you to do some work on your own and research all of the schools. You can find pretty much anything online or in brochures you can request, as well as at the college rep visits mentioned above. Once you feel like you have a good understanding of what schools can offer you, then you can start the process of narrowing them down.

GETTING ORGANIZED FOR THE PROCESS

- Get a box and start collecting info on colleges

- Figure out what you want to do in terms of degrees, possible jobs

- Start thinking about locations of colleges and planning out timelines for applying

- Meet with a college consultant, like an amazing coach at Elite Private Tutors

HOW TO HANDLE YOURSELF WHEN COLLEGES VISIT

- Dress your best

- Shake hands and get the info of every presenter

- Read about the school for a minimum of 1 hour prior to the presentation

- Come up with 5 questions: 3 specific to that college and 2 generic questions

- Write a handwritten card thanking them for their time and coming to your school. Mail it within 3 days of the presentation.

EARLY DECISION, DEADLINE IS IN THE NEXT 30-60 DAYS

....

The time has come. You're a senior, and you are going to start applying to colleges sooner than you know. Hopefully over the summer you started researching different schools and made a large list of schools that you're interested in, but since applications are due any minute now, it's time to narrow down that list. Since you have a general idea of the things each school has to offer, it is extremely helpful to rank them based on how well they fit what you're looking for.

Some important things to consider

- Does the school offer the field of study you think you're interested in?

- Are there clubs and organizations that you wish to continue in, or start if the school does not offer them?

- Does the school have Greek life (sororities and fraternities)?

- What are the acceptance rates to graduate programs that you might be interested in (i.e. medicine, law, etc.)?

- How far away from home is the school?

- Do you have other friends looking to go to the same school?

- What size school do you want?

- Public versus Private?

Of course, there are many, many more things to consider. Once you think of all the factors that are important to you personally, is there one school that very clearly stands out as the perfect school for you? If there is, you should do a little bit more research and figure out if they have the option to apply Early Decision or Early Action.

Basically, Early Decision admission programs allow you to figure out where you're going way before all of your friends that applied the regular way. This means you will have bragging rights and can start all of the shopping for your college dorm rooms way earlier than everyone else.

So I haven't really explained to you what Early Decision is. Basically, if you apply ED, you are telling the school that if you are accepted, you are 100% committed to going there. If you get accepted, you're forced to withdraw your applications from all other schools and, like I said, commit 100% to the school which you applied ED. The admissions team really likes to see students apply this way because it shows that you are whole-heartedly invested in their school. That being said, it's still a wise choice to apply to at least a few other schools, because there is still the chance you won't get in.

Perks of applying early decision

- Getting the application process done sooner (by three months).

- Having bragging rights over your friends when you know where you're going to college before all of them (they tell you early).

- Peace of mind and more time to prepare.

- Looking like a committed student to the admissions committee.

College application checklist

- Essays completed and crafted.

- Application completed.

- Resume (1-2 pages long).

- Teacher recommendations (1 or 2, depending on the college).

- Test scores submitted.

- Copy of mailed application.

- Handwritten card to admission counselor.

HOW TO APPLY EARLY ACTION AND REGULAR DECISION

....

You've done the college visits, and now it is finally time to sit down and start applying to colleges. You look at the deadlines for when an application for a certain college that you want to attend is due, and find that there are two different due dates. One of the deadlines is for early action, while the other is a regular registration deadline. It is a MUST that you turn in your application before the deadline for early action.

Do not take the easy way out and procrastinate until the last minute to turn in a half-assed application and meet the regular registration deadline. One of the reasons to apply early action to a college is that you receive many of the same benefits of applying early decision, but the non-binding nature of early action allows you to compare multiple college options and not be stuck with just one college option. Additionally, applying early action reduces the stress of having to wait months for a decision. I remember that I had applied to 8 different colleges regular decision, and unfortunately had to hear from all of them on the same day. Plus, most colleges have rolling admissions, so the earlier you are, the more invested you appear.

Had I applied early action, I definitely believe the constant stress of wondering if I would be accepted to a college would have been drastically reduced. I was definitely jealous of many of my peers, who had applied early action and had gotten accepted into a college in February. They appeared much more relaxed, as if a huge weight had been lifted off their shoulders. Applying early action, in my opinion, also shows the college that you are very interested in attending their institution, and may in fact give you a higher chance of getting accepted. Early action deadlines are in November, and regular decision is in December or January.

In summary

- Applying early action increases your chances of getting in.

- Reduces the stress of having to wait months for a regular decision (sometimes you can get deferred on waiting lists, which means that you end up waiting until May).

- Don't procrastinate when writing your applications (start at least three months earlier).

- Colleges you apply early action to will like that you are very interested in their institution.

- Regular decision is always an option, but you will hear later from the admissions counselors.

HOW TO CRAFT THE PERFECT ESSAY

· ·

Unfortunately for many of you, you think your college essays should match your high school essays. Throw that out the window. Your essay needs to be closer to a provocative news article with edgy language or a private journal entry.

Admissions counselors want to peer into your heart and soul. They know your brain's capabilities through your test scores and your GPA. They want to get deep with you. Here is my list of ideas for a personal statement essay. Talk about:

- What you stand for.

- The lessons learned in high school.

- Something you might not even want your parents to read.

- Personal hardship.

- An inspirational person or what you are passionate about.

- An international experience.

Suggestions for your structure

- Be very to the point. They read it in under 2 minutes.

- Be concise. Stay under the word limit or shorter.

- Use imagery or descriptive words.

- Hook the reader with the first sentence.

- Personalize your essay at the end by mentioning that you would love to attend X school in Fall of X!

- Use paragraphs – roughly 2 or 3.

- Write in a personal style and not English paper style.

Topics you want to avoid

- Being captain of the football or cheerleading team.

- Your pet.

- How much you hated school.

- Vague topics that you actually don't care about.

- Your grades.

- Your crazy Spring Break trip.

- Or anything on a superficial level for that matter!

Remember, your essay can literally make or break your application! Crack yourself and open to the reader!

HOW TO AVOID SENIORITIS

You can see the light at the end of the tunnel—you're almost there! But let's not forget that you have another semester to get through before you can celebrate being done. Senioritis is hard to avoid, because you've put in so much time and effort to get here that now you just want to sit back and admire your hard work. We get it. Now that your applications are in, why should anyone care what you do with your time now?

Cruising through your last semester, however, will not look cool to colleges, and it definitely won't help prepare you for your next year of study. Many students forget, or maybe just don't know, that colleges can actually retract offers of admission if your GPA or academic performance drops in your last semester. They want students who can finish strong, and senioritis proves that you won't be that student.

Furthermore, this last semester is your last chance to actually prepare for academic life in college. It's your last chance to test out your study strategies, your organizational skills, and your time management. I can tell you now, your academic studies will only get tougher from here on out - and if you take a semester off from academic discipline this spring, you will be in for a rude awakening. It will be that much harder to get back into your good habits for college.

I'm not saying don't do anything but study your senior year. It's your last semester, you should enjoy the time you have left with your friends, and attend all of the silly and fun activities that you can. But you can do that without completely giving up on your schoolwork. For the rest of your life, you will have to balance work and play, and for the next four years, social time and school time. You may as well start practicing your balancing act now, because you will be that much more prepared for your future.

Additionally, the bad habits that you develop your second semester of senior year may actually carry over to your freshmen year of college, and can harm your academic career in college. Senior year is supposed to help you academically transition from high school to college. From experience, I did not try as hard as I could have my second semester of my senior year, and then I was rewarded with a four-month summer vacation where I barely did anything productive at all. Thus, choice set me up for a rude awakening my first semester of freshmen year at Rice, because I had not practiced good study habits for 6 to 7 months.

At Rice, I was blindsided by the difficulty of the classes, and I appeared to have forgotten how to study due to the senioritis that I had developed during my senior year. It took me a semester at Rice to remember just how much hard work was required to successfully perform in a class.

Lastly, I would recommend against developing senioritis because of the legacy that you leave behind at your high school. Your teachers may lose respect for you when they realize that you have the mental capacity to perform much better in class, but you choose not to do so because you are too lazy to put in the work. Also, AP courses happen in this semester. Top scores can help you to gain college credit and cover your tuition bill by fulfilling requirements!

Why senioritis is bad

- Symptoms of senioritis include laziness, skipping classes, and lack of studying.

- High school is a transition toward college, so it is important to practice your studying habits in high school.

- How you study in high school translates to how you study in college, and slacking off in high school may hurt you in college.

- Teachers may lose respect for you when they realize you are not trying as hard as possible in their classes.

- You could have offers from colleges retracted.

HOW TO RELAX

....

I know, we told you to avoid senioritis, and now we are telling you to relax! But you've done it. You've overcome the most stressful part about senior year. All your college apps are in, you recently started a new semester, and you may have even already received an acceptance letter or two.

So, now what do you do? This past year has probably been one of the most stressful ones in your life so far. Unless you are a Nobel prize-winning researcher at the age of 18, you have probably never done so much work in such a short amount of time. Between all of the essays, recommendation letters, applications, and scholarship applications, you barely found time to eat, sleep, and study for your classes. What's next?

It may seem unnatural to you to have all of this free time available. Your first instinct at this point may be to make yourself busy again. After all, you're not doing anything right now, so you must have forgotten to complete some other application, right? Stop. Don't get stressed out again. You have finally been given a well-deserved break.

Around February of your senior year, things will start to slow down immensely. While your classes should just be picking up again, compared to the whirlwind of last semester, they will be a walk in the park.

Well... almost. Senior year is still not completed. You still have to finish your upper-level courses and graduate—otherwise, all the work that you have put in will have been for nothing. However, you should slow down a little bit, and take advantage of the time you have to relax.

RELAX, I'm telling you. It may seem bizarre and awkward at first to have nothing to do, but soon enough you will come to embrace and love the time you have to yourself. Enjoy it while it lasts! In a few months you will have to start making decisions about your future, and these are ones that cannot be made in one night. This month is all about putting aside your worries and de-stressing. It is also a great month to invest in yourself. Invest in your skills, relationships, and happiness. Take up a new hobby. You will be amazed at how the process of learning a new skill can calm you and boost your confidence.

One thing I started doing when I was a senior was learning how to play Ultimate Frisbee. I met up with a friend every afternoon, and we practiced all of our throws and catches. Not only did I feel better about myself for mastering a new skill, I would also later use that skill to play Ultimate Frisbee competitively in college. If sports aren't your thing, try undertaking some sort of creative or personal project. Pick a long book you have always wanted to read and make that your goal for the next month. Engage your mind in a fun and compelling goal, so that you will lift your sense of self-worth and rejuvenate your energy levels.

This part of your year should be fun! Try to distance yourself from potential stressors. Do NOT excessively check your email and mail for acceptances/denial letters from colleges. Doing so will build up anticipation and worry, preventing you from completing your "detox" month. Keep yourself mildly occupied, and take your mind off colleges and your future for a while.

If the opportunity presents itself, or you are simply too much of a busy bee that doing nothing stresses you out more than it helps you, look up and complete a few scholarship applications. Don't make this your after-school job, however, at least not yet. It's vital that you allow your mind to recuperate from all the work that you put it through.

Recap of what to do this month

- RELAX.

- Take up a new hobby or skill. This can be trying to learn a new sport, or starting some sort of month-long personal project.

- Do a little bit of work on scholarships, but don't let this consume your life.

- Put aside stressors and focus on the "now."

- Don't be afraid to have fun!

HOW TO DECIDE ON A CAREER – YES, THERE IS LIFE AFTER COLLEGE

....

The process of getting into college can be stressful and time-consuming, especially if you're shooting for highly selective, elite universities. Often students focus so much on this stage that they start to think of 'getting in' as the end goal, or the finish line for the race they've been running since elementary school. Most chapters of this book discuss the steps students should take during high school to maximize their chances of getting into the college of their choice, and to prepare them for the rigors of college life. It is important to remember, however, that college itself is primarily a means to another end - it's a means of learning the skills necessary to get a job, and excel at the career of your choice. It is also a means of networking with current and future colleagues in your chosen field. To most effectively utilize the opportunities college provides, you need to have a clear picture of the goal you are working toward: your future career.

Making the most of your college experience (and tuition money) requires you to be goal-oriented from your first day on campus, if not before. After getting used to the rigid nature of a high school curriculum, many new college students will find themselves faced with a 'choice overload.' Suddenly there are hundreds of classes to choose from, your study and degree plans are largely up to you, and dozens of interesting extracurricular organizations are competing for your membership. On top of that, the constant social opportunities that result from thousands of unsupervised young people living in one place can provide a powerful distraction. Most students naturally want to try everything, but there just isn't time. It helps tremendously to know what you are working toward.

Exploring career options in college is both common and encouraged, but it helps to have a head start on understanding yourself and your goals before you get there, so as not to get overwhelmed by the aforementioned 'choice overload.' Thinking carefully about your strengths, weaknesses, goals, and desires while still in high school can not only steer you in the right direction, but also make you a stronger candidate in the long run. Gaining relevant work or observational experience outside the high school classroom can give you a better idea of what it is like to work in a particular field, and it also helps build a strong resume early on, even if you don't end up pursuing work in that field. I had internships every Summer of high school.

In addition, choosing your "dream college" is heavily dependent on the type of degree you want to get. Even the most elite universities have departments and degree programs that are much more prestigious than others. The earlier you do your research, the earlier you can decide if a school or career path is truly right for you. It's easier and more effective to take care of this in high school, before you've made any lasting commitments.

HOW DO I DECIDE?

Choosing a career path is a big decision. They say the average person changes careers five times. It's comforting to know you aren't the only indecisive person out there, but wouldn't it be nice to get it right the first time? Or at least early enough to have a long, fruitful career with minimal setbacks? The trouble is, it's much easier to find advice on how to get from point A to point B than it is to find advice on how to choose where your own 'point B' will be located. Choosing a career isn't as simple as deciding how much money you want to make, or finding what you're 'best at.' No, it's about finding the calling that makes you feel happy and most fulfilled—something that is much harder to nail down than a salary or a talent. Some people just know what they want to be when they grow up, but a lot of us have to step back and honestly consider our talents and aspirations before we can point our efforts in the proper direction.

With that in mind, here are some steps you can take to zero in on your ideal career path.

Academic performance

Before you set out exploring the myriad career options out there, it's important to honestly assess yourself. One obvious place to start is with your grades thus far in high school. The one-size-fits-most class structure of high school can make classes seem overly abstract and detached from real-world employment situations. After all, few people go on to become English professors or mathematicians. Even so, the skills you learn in English and Math class can turn out to be applicable in certain career environments.

While grades are the logical first step in your self-assessment, it's important to remember that at this point, they aren't determinative of your career's destiny. Good high school grades can give you a hint of where your career talent lies, but so-so ones might just mean that you need to put more effort into developing certain skills if you want to succeed in a profession that requires them. From there, it's a question of your motivation.

Beyond what your grades say about your performance in a subject area, it's also important to consider your enjoyment of that subject. Remember that a career isn't just about being good at something—it's about loving something enough to spend the better part of your life working on it. You may have gotten an excellent grade in Calculus, but are you willing to spend a career modeling physical processes with equations as an engineer? This is more difficult than looking at the numbers on a report card, but an honest assessment of what motivates you will pay dividends in the long run.

Career aptitude testing

Grades can tell you a lot about your academic strengths and weaknesses, but it's enormously helpful to think beyond what you've done so far in class and understand on-the-job demands before you can plan confidently for your future. Career aptitude tests provide an easy way to gain a more holistic perspective on your talents as they relate to particular career fields. There are several useful aptitude tests to choose from, many of them created by universities and leading test prep companies. These tests help you match your interests and personality traits to the characteristics associated with success in various career fields. Even the best aptitude test can't truly zero in on the perfect career for you (and a good one won't claim to), but they can tell you a lot about your talents and provide a useful list of career suggestions to serve as a starting point in your exploration.

Hobbies

Another useful piece of your self-assessment is your hobbies and extracurricular activities. From playing an instrument to carpentry to watching movies, hobbies can often provide insight into the interests that motivate you. If you enjoy something enough to spend your free time cultivating a talent for it, you'd probably enjoy incorporating it into paid work. Seeing your career the way you see a hobby makes it easier to dedicate the significant time and energy required for success in most professions.

Career counselor

Once you have a better picture of your talents and aspirations, the next step is to explore career options. More unique career opportunities exist than any list could contain, but there are plenty of resources out there to help focus your research. Instead of hopping on the Internet and venturing out on your own, it's better to go to your high school or university career counselor and speak to them about what you've learned in your self-assessment.

A career counselor can prove to be an invaluable tool by giving you a more thoughtfully tailored list of career suggestions than an aptitude test, as well as access to resources for further exploration. A counselor can also guide you through the process of preparing for a particular career, explaining degree or certification requirements and suggesting universities that have notable programs in the field. The counselor may also be able to put you in contact with a community member working in the field to provide more insight, or serve as a mentor. These career counselors can usually provide you with all the resources you need to confidently explore your options.

Insider perspective

Once a counselor has helped you focus your career research and given you resources to conduct your own independent inquiry, it's time to dig into the dirty details of careers that pique your interest. The best way to find out what a career is like is to get involved with it directly. Classes related to a career don't always show what working in the field is really like, even college-level courses. On the other hand, talking to or working under someone in the position you're considering can expose you to aspects of the career and its lifestyle that aptitude tests and counselors cannot give you insight into.

Talk to your parents or your career counselor about meeting a professional in the field you are considering. There's a good chance that you are only a degree or two away from someone in this position, and an even better chance that they are willing to share their experiences with you. Talking with a professional allows you to get a 'second opinion' on what working in that field is like, only in this case you have the opportunity to ask questions about aspects you won't necessarily find in reading materials. Such as, how different is the reality of the career from the way it is stereotyped in movies and TV shows? What qualities have made the person successful at their job? What are the biggest challenges, both professional and personal, of working in this field? What drew them to this profession, and what do they perceive as its biggest reward? Interviewing a professional this way allows them to candidly share just why it is that they do what they do, which in turn allows you to analyze their motivations and compare them to your own.

Interviewing a professional also helps you find out about a critical but often overlooked aspect of entering a career field: the limitations it places on your lifestyle out of the office. Just as important as learning about the job itself is learning about the demands it will place on other aspects of the life you want to lead. First, think of life goals and aspirations you have that are unrelated to your career. Do you want to have kids? Do you want to be heavily involved in their development? Do you want to maintain your current hobbies and friendships? Next, consider what your 'insider' has told you about their lifestyle and decide if the career is compatible with your preferred lifestyle. Will the work/life balance allow you to meet your lifestyle goals and find fulfillment? Will the projected compensation be enough to build your ideal life and pursue your hobbies? Are there similar professions you might like to work in, that are more compatible with your preferred lifestyle? Even if you find the answer to some of your questions is 'no,' you shouldn't necessarily shy away from pursuing that career. You simply have to balance your desire to work in that field against your other lifestyle goals, and decide what is most valuable to you.

If you decide to commit to further pursuit of your career after learning more about it from an 'insider,' the next step is to find a mentor who can give you firsthand advice on how to proceed. This could be the same person you've already interviewed, or another person in the profession. A mentor with experience in the field has the benefit of hindsight, and they can give you advice based on what they've seen work, as well as what they wish they'd done when they were in your shoes. This information can allow you to get your best possible head start on the career of your dreams.

Get involved early on

Once armed with the advice of your mentor, it's never too early to get direct, hands-on experience working in the field. Even in high school, opportunities exist that can allow you work closely with a professional in your chosen field and observe their day-to-day activities. Opportunities might take the form of an internship or an entry-level, part-time job, many of which can be found through Internet research, your career counselor, or even directly through your mentor. Working in the field at any level not only give you hands-on experience to inform your career decisions, it also allows you to build a solid resume of relevant work experience early on. This in turn will give you a strong advantage in your search for college internships and post-college employment, should you decide to seriously pursue the career.

Get out there and explore

Settling on a career you can commit to isn't easy, at least not for everyone. There are endless factors to consider about strengths, limits, and desires, and it's inevitable that you will second-guess yourself along the way. The wisest course of action is to arm yourself with as much information as possible!

AP EXAMS

....

Advanced Placement (AP) examinations are taken each May by students in the United States. The tests are the results of year-long Advanced Placement courses. They include multiple-choice questions as well as a free-response section (either an essay or problem-solving).

Decisions on grading AP tests are made by the Chief Reader (a college or university faculty member selected by the College Board and the Educational Testing Service), along with a committee. The Chief Reader's decision is based upon the following criteria:

- What percentage of students earned each AP grade over the previous three years.

- How students did on multiple-choice questions that are used on the tests from year to year.

- How they viewed the overall quality of the answers to the free response questions

- The results of university students who took the exam as part of an experimental study.

- How students performed on different parts of the exam.

The AP grades that are reported to students, high schools, colleges, and universities in July are on a five-point scale:

- 5: Extremely well qualified

- 4: Well qualified

- 3: Qualified

- 2: Possibly qualified

- 1: No recommendation

The average score on all AP exams is slightly below a 3 (a 2.89 in 2013). In 2013, on more than 3 million AP exams administered, the grades were as follows:

- 5 - 14.3% of test takers

- 4 - 19.9% of test takers

- 3 - 24.7% of test takers

- 2 - 22.2% of test takers

- 1 - 18.8% of test takers

The bad news is that although the College Board defines a student obtaining 2 as "possibly qualified" to receive college credit, almost no college will accept a score of 2. In fact, most selective colleges will not even accept a 3 for college credit. Some schools actually require a 4 or 5.

However, in the majority of cases, a student who scores a 4 or 5 will receive college credit. The exact guidelines vary from college to college, and they often vary from department to department within a college. Make sure to do this research while applying to schools, as depending on which school you pick, you could enter as a sophomore or as a freshman. I entered into college as a sophomore, which made it easy to finish in 3 years!

Taking AP classes offers many perks. They'll allow you to:

- Impress college admissions counselors! Always remember that your academic record is the most important part of your college application. If the admissions committee sees that you challenged yourself with the hardest courses available, and you rocked them, I'm pretty sure they'll welcome you with open arms.

- Develop your academic skills. Your critical thinking and high-level calculating skills will definitely be an asset to start the next year.

- Save money. If you are not receiving financial aid or any other support, AP classes actually allow you to graduate early from college. That means saving thousands of dollars.

- Help you with your major. You'll get to know and understand things that other students around you won't be familiar with.

Taking AP classes will give you in-depth introductions to specific subject areas. Also, your high score on an AP exam may fulfill one of a college's education requirements. In other words: more room in your busy schedule to explore various academic fields!

GRADUATION

You did it! Soak in this moment, as it is one of the biggest accomplishments of the last four years of blood sweat. I want to end by sharing my high school commencement speech:

"To appreciate beauty, to find the best in others; to leave the world a bit better, whether by a healthy child, a garden patch, or a redeemed social condition; to know even one life has breathed easier because you have lived. This is to have succeeded." These words by Ralph Waldo Emerson have grown more relevant and meaningful over our years here at Episcopal High School.

I can honestly say that I am leaving Episcopal High School fulfilled, with a sense of true accomplishment. I am sad to leave this beautiful place that has been my home for four years, but I feel that I have grown so much and have been given numerous tools to move into the real world from the opportunities that Episcopal has given me. I feel that graduation is not a conclusion of our education, but a celebration of the journey we will embark on for the next four years.

One thing I found most important at Episcopal was to be a sponge. As students, we must immerse ourselves in new communities and become active members. As a freshman at EHS, I was given ample opportunities to participate in activities I felt passionate about. Through the Four Pillars - academics, religion, fine arts, and athletics, I was exposed to a multitude of new experiences. EHS also gave me the opportunity to be part of an active campus organization called Diversity in Action. I had never known of this type of organization, nor had I ever encountered other students who felt passionate about the same things I did. Through DIA and its sponsor, Mrs. Flores-Irwin, I found my niche and passion at Episcopal. My experience with DIA taught me to become a better public speaker, be more confident, empathize with others, and understand their backgrounds. EHS is a community of excellence in which diversity is not just tolerated, but embraced. Diversity takes effort – effort to learn about and respect differences, to be compassionate towards one another, and to cherish our own identities.

Also, my teachers stretched me throughout my four years at EHS and molded me into an active leader. I have developed from an uninvolved person to a woman who speaks her mind and involves herself totally in the EHS community. Through their inspiration, I have been able to reach a potential I could never dream of. Emerson's philosophy has permeated the EHS community as it strives to "find the best in others" and cultivates a secure and comfortable atmosphere for every student. By being part of this community of accomplished students, I have been inspired by many of my peers: students who helped me to believe in myself when I couldn't, students who gave me the vision to see my potential, and students with amazing abilities that generated energy and fire have inspired me to follow my own passion. Without this incredible group of students, my experience at Episcopal wouldn't have been the same. The Class of 2003 gave life to EHS through its enthusiasm and spirit.

The opportunities that EHS has offered us will be essential to our transition into college. EHS encourages its students to believe in something larger than their own lives. We will move into bigger environments, where we will face new challenges and responsibilities. We are all in a transitional period right now, between high school and college. Some of us are both anxious and exhilarated at having to make choices that will affect the rest of our lives. EHS has definitely made a lasting impression on us, and all of us have left our own imprints on EHS through our dedication and hard work.

We should remember that we are like clay. Although pressure may distort our appearance and cause weakness in our foundation, it can also mold us into better people. As people look at the holes, the marks, the blemishes in our clay-like structures, they won't see the negative, but instead, our elastic potential to mold ourselves into even better people.

Turn your wounds into wisdom. You will be wounded many times in your life. You'll make mistakes. Some people will call them failures, but failure is really just God's way of saying, "Excuse me – you're moving in the wrong direction." It's just an experience.

I would like to say congratulations to the Class of 2003. I have no doubt that all of us will make a very significant contribution to the world out there. As I look around today, I am confident you will make the right choices, because so many of you already have. Finally, I'd like to leave my class with one final message: As Ferris Bueller said on his day off, "Life moves pretty fast. If ya don't stop and look around once in a while, ya gonna miss it!"

LINKS

....

Elite Private Tutors • http://www.eliteprivatetutors.com

How to stay organized • http://tinyurl.com/ljmqnte

How to take notes • http://tinyurl.com/n684nec

How to get ready for back to school! http://tinyurl.com/l6xe8qf

Testimonial from a parent • http://tinyurl.com/m4kpgs7

Testimonial from a student • http://tinyurl.com/kvkd3x3

SAT Test Prep! • http://tinyurl.com/l8ms2pg

Get on your teacher's good side • http://tinyurl.com/qjf3tl9

How to understand progress reports http://tinyurl.com/k7zd3xt

Essay writing and paper tips • http://tinyurl.com/l4bk78j

FAFSA • https://fafsa.ed.gov

Financial aids you can get • http://www.fastweb.com

Career Aptitude Test • http://www.yourfreecareertest.com

How we do College Consulting • http://www.eliteprivatetutors.com